# 101010 **101** 010101010101
# MICRO-COMPUTER PROJECTS
## TO DO IN YOUR LIBRARY

*Putting Your Micro to Work*

*PATRICK R. DEWEY*

## AMERICAN LIBRARY ASSOCIATION
*Chicago and London 1990*

Cover and text designed by Charles Bozett.

Composed by ALA Books on a BestInfo Wave4 pre-press system and
output on a Linotronic L-300 in Times Roman
and Helvetica by Anzo Graphics.

Printed on 50-pound Glatfelter B-31, a pH-neutral stock, and bound in
10-point Carolina cover stock by Versa Press.

The paper used in this publication meets the minimum requirements of American National Standard
for Information Sciences—Permanence of Paper for Printed Library Materials, ANSI Z39.48-1984.
∞

Library of Congress Cataloging-in-Publication Data

Dewey, Patrick R., 1949–
    101 microcomputer projects to do in your library : putting your micro to work / Patrick R. Dewey.
        p.   cm.
    Bibliography: p.
    Includes indexes.
    ISBN 0-8389-0518-8
    1. Microcomputers—Library applications—Computer programs.   2. Library science—Computer
programs.   3. Libraries—Automation.   I. Title.   II. Title: One hundred one microcomputer projects to do in your library.       III. Title: One hundred and one microcomputer projects to do in your
library.
    Z678.93.M53D488   1989
    025. 17'4—dc20                                                            89-6957

This book is for

Ted Mercer

good friend for many years past
and for many yet to come

# Contents

Acknowledgments  ix

Introduction  xi

Projects and Their Management  1

The Projects  7

Acquisitions  8
  Automated Acquisitions Micro System  8
  Acquisitions Processing with *AppleWorks*  10
  *dBase III* for Acquisitions Department Budgeting  11

Bibliography Generation  12
  Spanish Bibliographies with *Bibliography Writer*  12
  Motivating Reading with Bibliographies on a Macintosh  13
  Bibliographies on a Macintosh  14

Budgeting and Accounting: Adding It All Up  16
  *dBase* for Expenditures in a University Library  16
  Budget Preparation Using Spreadsheets  17
  Automating the Book Budget  18

Bulletin Boards: Reaching Out to the World  20
  North–Pulaski BBS  21
  Wellspring BBS  22
  Lincolnet BBS  23
  Online Catalog and Bulletin Board  24

Circulation  26
  Overdues on a Macintosh  26
  Automated Circulation System  26
  Videotape List  27
  *Circulation Plus* in a School Library  28
  Software Lending  29
  Corporate Library Circulation System  30
  Special Library Circulation File; Routing Periodicals  32
  Videocassette Control  33

Automated Circulation System  34
*AppleWorks* Circulation System  34
Software Lending  35

## Desktop Publishing and Graphics  37

Creating Fliers on a Macintosh  37
Poster Production  38
Library Tour Using *HyperCard*  39
Newsletter and Calendar Production  39
Desk Schedules  40
Computerized Typesetting  41
Publishing a Newsletter on a Macintosh  42
Community Resource Directory  43
Desktop Publishing: "Golden Years Directory"  43
Retrospective Conversion on a Microcomputer  44

## Government Documents Control  46

Government Documents and Micros  46
Government Documents Processing System  47
Government Documents Keyword Indexing  47

## Handicapped Access  49

Special Needs Center  49

## Indexing  51

Local History (Newspaper Index)  51
Pamphlet Database  53
Vertical File  53

## Interlibrary Loan  55

ILL Data Collection  55
ILL Journal Request File  56
ILL Use of an Electronic Bulletin Board System  56

## Local Area Networks  58

LAN in a Hospital Library  58
Library Circulation and Inventory on a LAN  60

## Management  62

Salary Increases Using a Microcomputer  62
Maintaining Subscriber Files  62
Space Planning and Collection Analysis with *Enable*  63
Stack Management  64
Local History Collection Survey  65

## Online Catalogs and Catalog Cards  67

Catalog Cards  67
Computerized Media Catalog  68
Online Catalog for Media Center  69
MARC Record Staff Development Program  71
Statewide CD-ROM Union Catalog  72

Specialized Information Center 73
Media Catalog 74
AV Catalog Produced from Database 75

## Online Search Management 77
Working with Downloaded Medline Search Results 77
DIALOG Searching with a Macintosh 78
OCLC on a Macintosh 79
Search Statistics with *dBase III+* 80

## Output Measures 82
Patron Count Analysis 82

## Public Access Microcomputers 84
Walk-in Microcomputer Use 84
Public Access in a Tiny Branch Library 85
Loaning Microcomputers 86
Loaning Software in a Special Library 87
Walk-in Public Access 88
Public Domain Circulation 89
Workshops and Seminars 90
Circulating Public Domain Software 91
Macintosh Computers for Public Use 92
Microcomputer Center for Adults 92

## Reading Projects and Clubs 94
Summer Reading Club 94

## Reference 96
Automated Periodical Reference Service 96
Local Table of Contents 97
Subject Guide Wall Chart 98

## Serials Control 100
Serials Lists 100
Periodicals Management with *AppleWorks* 101
Periodicals Management Using a Macintosh 102

## Student and Patron Assistance and Training 104
Résumé Preparation for Patrons 104
Computer Fair Organizing 105
Young Adult Career Guidance 106
Computerized Career and Information Center 107
CD-ROM Electronic Encyclopedia 108
End-User Searching with CompuVend 109
Literacy 110

## Systems 112
In-House Integrated Library System 112
Multi-Campus Library Automation 113
Integrated Library System 114

Model Library Utilizing Microcomputers  115
Inventory and Union List of Libraries  117

User's Network  119
Microaide User's Network  119

Miscellany  121
Training Staff with a Microcomputer  121
Creating a Library User Group  122
Service for Faculty (Checkoutable Micro)  123
Streamlining Repetitive Tasks  124
Sheet Music Index  124
Statewide Referral Database  126
Cataloging Sound Recordings  127

Appendix A: Sample Project Proposal  129
Appendix B: Vendor List  133
Glossary of 101 Important Terms  137
Bibliography of Library Software Applications  143
Index of Project Sites  147
Index of Applications and Software  149

# Acknowledgments

I'd like to thank many people for making this book possible. First and foremost, there are those who took the time to answer yet another questionnaire. I hope they find their projects represented fairly and that readers find their work useful, even exemplary.

I also wish to thank the librarians at Apple Computer, Marvin Garber (Sulzer Regional, Chicago Public Library) for his helpful comments and project information, and the staff at the Merriam Center Library (Chicago), where a revolution in the use of the library Macintosh is under way.

# Introduction

This volume is a guide to microcomputer use in libraries. It does not center upon software or hardware, but rather on applications—specific, individual projects. Each project used hardware and software, of course, but most of them could have been done with many different types of software packages on many different computers. More important is the fact that libraries found these tasks or systems worth automating, and succeeded in doing so.

Contained within are accounts of projects involving online catalogs, bulletin board systems, desktop publishing, handicapped accessibility, indexes, local area networks, bibliographies, fliers and desk schedules, collection analysis, relocation of book collections, staff training using a micro, and much more. If nothing else, this volume affirms the widespread usefulness of the microcomputer in the library.

At another level, several entries discuss using a micro to organize a library user group to promote the continuous exchange of information between colleagues. Additional material explains how to conduct a hardware and software survey of libraries in order to acquire valuable information.

## Methods

Several good efforts have been made in the past to document the different library projects utilizing microcomputers. Most of these, however, have provided simple narratives that rarely go into any detail. To access a substantial number of carefully examined projects, readers have always been forced to conduct time-consuming literature searches. In the interests of ease and speedier access, this volume documents (as fully as possible) 101 actual projects—ranging from simple tasks to complete system replacements, from the single library to cooperative efforts by groups of libraries or state libraries.

In order to reflect a wide scope, many areas in which micros have proved useful in libraries were identified and then grouped accordingly. The next step was to find projects that represented these areas and perhaps even some areas that had not been originally considered.

Most projects were located in the literature, with the assumption that, for the most part, they would be well enough along to warrant sharing with others. This also meant, to some degree, that the librarians involved had to be willing to share information as well as organize it in an effective manner. Once 101 separate projects that fit the predetermined categories had been located, each project leader was identified and a pertinent address located.

A three-page survey of questions was mailed. The response was amazingly high, over 80 percent. Additional projects were then identified when it became apparent that no survey (or number of requests) was going to score a 100 percent response.

The basic information was nearly always self-evident. Occasionally there was difficulty in the "What Did You Do?" section of the survey, as some contributors merely assumed that the answers were obvious. (A better-constructed survey form might have alleviated this problem.) In any case, between the literature search, the surveys, and some follow-up phone calls, almost all data eventually were clarified, and the writing of the project descriptions could begin.

# Hardware and Software Selection

Most of the hardware cited in this book was purchased for reasons other than the projects at hand. It was simply pressed into service because it was available.

Software was selected for basically two reasons: the library already owned it (and it worked well), or the decision was based upon recommendations or reviews of software in the literature.

Sometimes, staff did the work on their own computers with their own software and on their own time.

Surprisingly, a large number of librarians used non-library-specific (generic) software such as *dBase*, which, in fact, often requires a great deal of programming time and skill. In addition, many libraries were quite content to do marvelous things with capable, yet simple-to-operate, software such as *AppleWorks*.

# How to Use This Book

This volume offers case-study materials. Each entry presents, as fully as possible, the essential facts (project goal, hardware and software used, etc.), the name of the contact person who organized and implemented the project, (along with address and telephone number) and, most importantly, the details of execution (project description followed by major problems, if any). A library profile is often included.

If this book had to be categorized, it would be considered "a book of ideas." This is especially true since it is easy for readers to browse the text searching for projects that might benefit their own libraries. Furthermore, each case study is intended as a modest blueprint. Whenever possible, potential stumbling blocks are pointed out to help those who might attempt a similar project. Readers should always remember: No two libraries are exactly the same, and therefore, no two projects will ever be exactly alike.

While some of the respondents reported no significant problems, I suspect that many of them had significant expertise and so, like the person doing a trapeze act, they made it look easy when it wasn't. Project dates, funding sources, and self-ratings are also included, the latter a strictly subjective factor based on a scale of 1 to 10. The reader may interpret this scale openly, since a large part of determining how well something goes will depend on how much work was involved, what was initially hoped to be achieved, etc. Some of the projects sound excellent, but might receive only a 5 or 6 on this scale. Readers may "take them or leave them."

# Projects and Their Management

## Project Management: An Outline

Computerizing some aspects of library work can be difficult. It includes assumptions about personnel, staff training, staff availability, etc. Essentials of the planning process include learning about microcomputers (hardware and software); talking with staff about the tasks or systems that the microcomputers might replace; and approaching systems logically, step by step. For instance, installing a simple catalog-card production system might incorporate the following activities:

1. Identifying the task or system to be computerized (in this case, making catalog cards).
2. Determining that the task needs to be computerized. (Will it be done more efficiently as a result of computerization?)
3. Discussing computerization, including the following questions:
   a. Who will be responsible for the equipment?
   b. How will staff be trained?
   c. Where will the equipment be housed?
   d. How will expendables such as paper and ribbons be housed?
   e. How will the equipment be repaired?
4. Selecting software. More than one person should evaluate catalog-card programs, while the entire staff should see at least some software demonstrated (and arrive at a consensus opinion on its applicability).
5. Selecting equipment, unless it is already in place (in which case software selection must be based on available equipment). In the case of catalog cards, it is necessary, for example, to consider a bottom-feed printer, which will accommodate heavy card stock.

## Needs Identification

What is worth computerizing? The answer to this basic question involves several steps: An examination of library procedures, and a meeting with appropriate staff, who can help to determine the needs and can pinpoint, in clear detail, why procedures don't work better. As part of the process, staff should be gradually oriented to the types of tasks that a computer system can automate. The ultimate groundwork for computerization is learning about microcomputers and what they can do—in other words, computer literacy.

## Software Selection

Software can be divided into categories—"generic," "do-it-yourself," and "library specific"—which illustrate some essential differences among packages. "Generic" software includes word processors, spreadsheets, and database managers. These programs are written for a wide range of applications and must be adapted accordingly. "Do-it-yourself" usually indicates a program packaged either from scratch (using BASIC or some other high-level language), or the use of a command language (programming language) that often is part of a major package, such as *dBase III+* or others. Such software provides for maximum flexibility since it can be reprogrammed in detail at any time. (It also requires some considerable expertise in programming.) "Library specific" software is created for specialized purposes such as catalog-card production. This type of software tends to be easy to use, though it is the least flexible and is difficult to customize for wider applications. The kind of software that should be selected will depend upon how much staff time is available for selection and programming, and, perhaps more importantly, how much staff expertise already exists.

Searching for a good piece of software can take some time. Here are a few basic tips.

1. Locate information about software packages that will do the job.
2. Compare packages.
3. Ask librarians who use various packages how well they like them.
4. Preview packages insofar as possible.

## Selection Criteria

Much has been written about the selection criteria for software; however several fundamental points should be stressed.

Software should be purchased for a specific task or system. It should be purchased based on its ability to interface with appropriate hardware and other software packages (i.e., compatibility, including the exchange of data files). Lastly, a list of necessary criteria should be compiled and compared with available software.

There are some general characteristics that are common to almost any software. These tend to be in the nature of the software itself, including such factors as speed of execution, quality of documentation, availability of backups, tutorials, online help files, vendor or manufacturer support (e.g., updates and telephone help), and ability to interface with other software packages.

One type of software not discussed above is the *template*. The template can take various forms, including the keyboard template, which is actually a cardboard or plastic overlay of commands that serves as a memory prompt. Template here, however, refers to documents or data sets (for spreadsheets) that represent prepared items that can be altered or changed to serve new purposes. For instance, a letter to a patron saved to disk may be retrieved from the disk and changed and sent on to a new patron. A spreadsheet template may represent work containing difficult formulas but that may be used anew by plugging in data for a new year or a different library, thus saving days of additional labor. (The Apple Library Users Group has produced a large volume of such templates covering hundreds of library applications. Write: Apple Library Users Group, 10381 Bandley Dr., Cupertino, CA 95014.)

Criteria for specific library software may become quite esoteric or complicated, and evaluation may only be possible, ultimately, through an examination of the product. For example, a circulation package may require bar-coding of an entire collection before a single book can be checked, or it may not permit the use of a bar-code wand—important distinctions.

Some of the tools needed in this endeavor are software directories and reviews of software. Since most library software is ordered through the mail, it can be difficult to see it in use before actual purchase. Some companies do offer either demo packages or permit software to be sampled and then returned within a specified time if is not satisfactory.

## User Groups

User groups comprise people who get together to share hardware or software information—in person, through the mail, through magazines or newsletters, or electronically. Such groups have been in existence for at least ten years and serve a useful purpose. In addition to discussing hardware and software, they may also share ideas about applications. Librarians considering the purchase of software packages may find user groups an ideal source for knowledge about particular packages. In the event that no user group serving a library orientation is available in a given region, librarians may create their own user network by taking an inventory of hardware and software and applications via a simple questionnaire. Once the data are compiled and mailed to local users, an extremely useful network of contacts for librarians can be established. Many systems and even state libraries have done this exact thing.

## Hardware Selection

There are three excellent machines that libraries generally choose for microcomputer projects: Apple, IBM (or clone), or Macintosh (an Apple tradename).

While it is possible to perform a majority of the projects on any of these, there is a lot to be said about enhancements, peripherals, and other devices that increase a computer's capabilities.

Hardware is, of course, the nuts and bolts of any operation. The monitor, the keyboard, the disk drives, the printer, the modem, and the central processing unit are all hardware. Ideally, when software is selected first, then the appropriate hardware should fall right into place. Unfortunately, life is not that simple, and the library may already own one type of equipment (and wish to maintain and repair and keep software for only that kind of machine). Budgetary considerations come into play, and not all equipment is easy on the pocketbook.

Peripherals (printers, disk drives, etc.), may actually be more expensive than the initial outlay for the computer itself. If, for example, top-quality desktop publishing is the goal, a laser printer will be required, and these can cost several thousand dollars or more. Special bottom-feed printers, used to accommodate heavy catalog-card stock, also tend to extract a premium from purchasers. A hard disk drive may not be expensive, but a large hard drive of 70–100 megabytes of storage—the basic unit of computer storage is the byte, one character, a megabyte being one million bytes— may cost a thousand dollars or more. If the computer (especially the Apple or the Macintosh) does not come with full internal RAM (random access memory), depending upon the application, it may be necessary to purchase more, which may cost hundreds of dollars extra.

The modem (from modulate-demodulate) is the computer's connection with the outside world, transforming the digital signals of the computer into the analog signal of the telephone system. A modem at the receiving end does the reverse. A capacity of 1200 baud (120 characters per second) is now common, but 2400 baud is rapidly becoming available to everyone, especially to those who transmit data that are not meant to be read online but only sent and received between two computers as quickly as possible to keep costs down. Once basic decisions have been made—the equipment and software ordered— there is still much to be done on an ongoing basis.

## Off and Running

Sometimes equipment arrives unannounced, like a baby on a doorstep. (One library administrator stated that a microcomputer was delivered to the library with no explanation. Eventually, it was discovered that a board member, impressed with micros at a conference, had one sent, without telling anyone until after the fact!) Usually, however, hardware is ordered by the library, though specific goals may not have been spelled out (i.e., when it arrives, no one really knows what it is supposed to do). In the best situation, equipment is expected, and a set of routines can begin immediately.

The first of these, of course, is set-up. Depending on the type of equipment and staff expertise, it may be necessary for internal hard drives, RAM, etc., to be installed by the local vendor. Printer interface with the computer can be difficult to attain, too, as can be the installation of the modem. Many peripherals have DIP (Dual In-Line Package) switches which allow for a state being on or off. For example, a certain DIP switch may force a line feed if activated.

It is unfortunate that this level of tasks can get so very complicated; it is perhaps the least forgiving aspect of computer technology. Users must simply persevere until the right combination of switches and default states has been made.

User manuals should document the location and function of switches as well as how to set things up. Attaching cables, outlet boxes, disk drives, surge protectors, etc., can often be accomplished simply by reading the directions. If not, many manufacturers provide ''800'' numbers for technical assistance. Local vendors may also help out. Do not hesitate to call them whenever necessary.

The equipment and manuals should all reside in the same place, a workstation. Several workstations are used if there is a local area network (LAN) in effect. Setting up a LAN is considerably more difficult, and in most cases, a consultant will be required, as will ready access to vendors and manufacturers.

## Protecting Equipment

Of course, things can go awry. Electrical charges in the form of surges or spikes can devastate a system, so it is advisable to purchase surge protectors and install them between the outlets and the equipment as a buffer. Static electricity can create problems for both machines and diskettes. Special anti-static sprays will help, as will special floor mats.

To guard against theft, bolt the equipment down, lock it up, or install electronic security. Or do all three.

## Staff Training

Training the staff can be a difficult chore, especially when trainees are unwilling, or fearful, or simply ''too busy'' to be bothered with this overpriced toy. If the staff can be led to believe that they have played a role in making the initial decisions, they may well feel compelled to make a good showing when it arrives.

## Steps in the Computerization Process—A Summary

The computerization process includes a number of distinct steps, from the initial brainstorming sessions to a formal and written plan, and should include input from a variety of people, installation of equipment, and a system for review of ideas and feedback.

1. The plan should outline what is to be computerized, who is to do it, what hardware and software will be used, etc.
2. Set-up. A properly equipped workstation, with lighting, supplies, and quiet, should be made available. Equipment should be set up by someone with experience or by the vendor.
3. Staff training and recruitment. Staff must be trained on the software and hardware, and new staff members must be given training as old staff members leave. These are essential to the health and future life of the project.
4. Liaison with staff. Someone must provide a direct line to the administrator or project manager. Staff must feel that their wishes are important and at least being given a hearing.
5. Volunteers can be useful for certain types of computer work, especially data entry. For instance, some seniors enjoy going through old local newspapers and indexing them, a task that would otherwise require much regular staff time.
6. Backup is a crucial aspect of computing. Work that has not been saved to disk may be lost if power fails. One disk can be easily destroyed or lost. Two disks, stored in separate locations, are safer, and three safer still.
7. Programming software from scratch may also require that changes be made to accommodate new features (or ''patches'' may be added to solve problems). Not to do either is to invalidate many of the reasons for programming software in the first place.
8. New software (updates and changes). Many projects find that the original software, though initially adequate, may not have been the best selection after all, and then opt for new software. Updates are a fact of life, and when offered by the vendor, they should be ordered and installed like new software. (Make sure that the new version is compatible with the old data.)
9. New hardware (change in system or peripherals). ''Add-on's'' can enhance the memory, speed, or other capability of the computer. A new laser printer can produce letter- and production-quality output. As prices fall on such devices, libraries will want to update hardware configurations to reflect the changing world.
10. Feedback and refinement respond to the need to see how well the entire project is going. If there is a set of objectives, including time frame, production schedules, tasks or systems to be computerized, etc., initial evaluations should not be difficult. Later, after the system is under way, periodic checks will be needed to determine adjustments to maintain or improve it.

# The Projects

The projects below represent the many ways librarians can use microcomputers in school, special, academic, and public libraries, including small, medium-sized, and large institutions. Above all, the projects show that there is always more than one effective way to accomplish the same goal. Some libraries have successfully programmed from scratch, some have used special command languages that are available in software such as *dBase IV*, and others have used specialized programs specifically intended for library use.

Equipment (or the lack thereof) rarely interfered with the librarians' ability to get things done. They simply worked harder when necessary. Not having access to the absolute latest technology is no excuse for inefficiency.

Just about every sort of activity in a library has now been automated to one extent or another: catalog card production, reference services, vertical file maintenance, inventory, circulation, special collection catalogs, and even tutoring library skills. I hope that this book may inspire those librarians not yet involved with microcomputers. It is hard to imagine that a newcomer cannot find good ideas from the many successful projects profiled in the pages that follow.

Quite a variety of hardware is represented, including the lowest-end Apple IIs, the Commodore 64, IBMs (and clones), the Macintosh, and other, less well-known brands. However hardware changes as time goes by, and the configurations that will be in use in two, three, or five years are impossible to predict. Nevertheless, I believe that one can count on a good mixture of machines and peripherals, perhaps more sophisticated, but still varied. That will provide the librarian with continued opportunities to experiment, to try new things. Sometimes we fail, but the longer view shows that success can only come when individuals see unique possibilities, get excited about them, and decide that they can find a way to apply them to library work. And that's what it's all about!

# Acquisitions

Acquisitions encompasses a great many tasks in a library, and it is handled differently in libraries of different sizes. A small library may only wish to keep an on-order file of materials, pulling titles as they arrive. Larger libraries may wish to systemize fund accounting, automate generation of purchase orders, etc. It can all be done in different ways, including buying simple packages that do only one thing, installing an entire system for handling a book from order to receipt, or programming with *dBase* or generic packages such as *AppleWorks* or *WordPerfect*.

## Further Reading

Desmarais, Norman. *Essential Guide to the Library IBM PC, Volume 11: Acquisitions Systems for Libraries*. Meckler, 1988. This volume provides a comprehensive look at many commercial acquisitions systems. "Microcomputer Circulation Control Systems: An Assessment," *Library Technology Reports*, Jan.–Feb. 1986.

| | |
|---|---|
| Name: | **Automated Acquisitions Micro System** |
| Library: | Health Sciences Library/SUNY at Buffalo |
| Contact Person: | Pamela M. Rose |
| Address/Phone: | 126 Abbott Hall, Buffalo, NY 14214; (716) 831-2408 |
| Profile: | This is a major biomedical library serving schools of medicine, nursing, health-related professions, dentistry, and pharmacy and affiliated teaching hospital staff. The annual monograph budget is approximately $150,000, with 4,000 new volumes added each year. The staff comprises approximately 30 FTEs. |
| Hardware: | Project began with a Tandy Model 16B, 15-megabyte hard drive. Changed in late 1987 to IBM PC/AT, with 20-megabyte hard drive, Okidata 192/193 printer, and Practical Peripheral internal modem. |
| Software: | *dBase II* (Ashton-Tate), upgraded later to *dBase III+*. |

Originally chosen because of flexibility and programming language (one of the few database systems at the time that had these properties). Plans call for upgrading to *dBase IV*. Staff has written approximately seventy *dBase* programs.

Description: This project continues to be developed and upgraded as required. It is a "do-it-yourself" project, meaning that the staff worked with the generic package, *dBase*, to create the required system. The resulting program, which holds about 7,000 records of 700 characters each, tracks all books ordered and received, including those on approval plan, gifts, and firm orders. Continuation orders are not presently included, but future expansion in this area is anticipated. Reports that can be generated include: monthly financial reports, count of orders placed, purchase-order copies for external vendors, a biweekly title and books-in-process listing for the reference desk, and quarterly production of new acquisitions list and newsletter. Other future plans include interfacing with a spreadsheet used for "prediction and control." A comparison of the new system and the old, manual system showed that processing time for orders was reduced by 33 percent. (It now takes approximately three seconds to retrieve any record on the hard disk drive.) Start-up and development times were considerable, but the finished product is highly customized for the library and can be altered at any time as needs change.

Significant Problems: Compatibility between the Tandy and IBM software was not 100 percent. One of the problems with the first effort was the unfriendly and difficult manner in which the software interfaced with the user. The second version has much more user-friendly menus. Only libraries with staff who can program (or who are willing to learn) should attempt this type of project. Furthermore such a project should be worked at in stages, looking ahead to potential compatibility with other systems and software. Up to six hours per day is spent doing backup and indexing chores. Such a system also calls for strict, step-by-step documentation—the creation of manuals—for the procedures.

Reference: None available

Project Date(s): September 1984–Present

Cost: Original Tandy, approximately $10,000; Newer PC/AT, about $5,000; software, about $1,000.

Self Rating: Not given

| | |
|---|---|
| Name: | **Acquisitions Processing with *AppleWorks*** |
| Library: | Brunswick–Glynn County Regional Library |
| Contact Person: | Terry Tench |
| Address/Phone: | 208 Gloucester St., Brunswick, GA 31520; (912) 267-1213 |
| Profile: | Staff consists of ten professionals and seventeen clerical. Holdings are approximately 200,000 volumes. The library serves a population of over 118,000, with a Talking Book Center, six branch libraries, and five bookmobiles. |
| Hardware: | Apple IIe, two 5-megabyte Profile hard drives, Imagewriter printer, 1.5-megabyte RamWorks card. |
| Software: | *AppleWorks* (Apple Computers) |
| Description: | This is a study in trial and error and in perseverance through several different software systems. The library needed a more efficient, computerized way to handle acquisitions processing, including catalog-card production, on-order file, and accounting. Originally starting with *QuickFile* (Apple Computers), which allowed too few fields, conversion to *DB Master* (Stoneware) followed, but, though an improvement, required masses of diskettes to handle very large files and was slow to sort, among other problems. A year later, *AppleWorks* was installed. While a big improvement, considerable time was required to evolve into the desired system. This electronic database replaced many paper forms, including order, bibliographic, and financial data storage forms, another form to provide the typist with necessary information, and a temporary form for the public service departments prior to book arrival and processing. *AppleWorks* flexibility makes such automation possible by providing a word processor for creating catalog cards and a database system for creating on-order and fund-accounting files. The database is extremely useful as a source for author, title, and subject indexes that would normally have to be found in the card catalog located some distance from the processing staff. Since the library staff used *AppleWriter* before *AppleWorks* became available, they elected to retain it because of some of its advanced features (e.g., the glossary function), especially useful for catalog-card production. The staff is also pleased with the clipboard and other functions of *AppleWorks*, which allow duplication of files or sections of files by moving data from one file to another. The system is still an evolving one that the staff modifies as necessary. Those interested in using *AppleWorks* in such a comprehensive way would do well to obtain Tench's lengthy article, cited below. |

Significant Problems:  See above

Reference:  *Apple Library Users Group Newsletter*, April 1986, p.36. This article describes the project in great detail, outlining how it began with *Quickfile* and progressed through *DB Master* and finally *AppleWorks*.

Project Date(s):  1982–Present

Cost:  $4,000 for equipment purchased for other purposes.

Self Rating:  9

Name:  ***dBase III* for Acquisitions Department Budgeting**

Library:  Atwood Library, Beaver College

Contact Person:  Lynne Meyers Hayman

Address/Phone:  Technical Services, Atwood Library, Glenside, PA 19038

Profile:  The Atwood Library serves a student body of about 1,200 and a faculty of 80. Library holdings exceed 113,000 volumes.

Hardware:  IBM PC (M300) with 20-megabyte hard-disk drive.

Software:  *dBase III+* (Ashton-Tate)

Description:  *dBase* has made it possible to assign the actual cost of books and periodicals to academic departments at Beaver College, where previously the cost for subscriptions had been allocated first, then remaining funds distributed for book purchases. The library is now able to determine precisely how money is being divided by subscription costs and book allocations. A database of two files—one containing active periodical titles and the other continuations—was created, containing subscription prices for each title as well as an assigned department code. The *dBase* report generator was used, requiring no additional programming by library staff, and copies of each department's share were distributed, with a request for evaluation of unwanted titles. Once updates were returned, the database was used to delete unwanted titles. Funds from all cancelled subscriptions became part of the book budget. In each new subscription cycle, this same process is repeated.

Significant Problems:  None reported

Reference:  None available

Project Date(s):  1985–86

Self-Rating:  Not given

# Bibliography Generation

Most libraries create bibliographies for one reason or another, often for distribution to the public as new-book or materials-holdings lists. Sometimes they are used by staff at the reference desk. In either case, the more efficiently they can be produced, the more useful they become.

Name: **Spanish Bibliographies with *Bibliography Writer***

Library: Maywood Public Library

Contact Person: Kristin Flanders

Address/Phone: 121 S. Fifth Ave., Maywood, IL 60153; (312) 343-1847

Profile: Maywood Public Library serves a community of approximately 28,000 residents, approximately 70 percent black, the remainder split between Hispanic and white. It has one branch library (storefront) and one main library.

Hardware: Apple IIe, 128K, Imagewriter II

Software: *Bibliography Writer* (Follett Software)

Description: Though books in Spanish are accessible through the online circulation system, a specialized local database of Spanish titles provides the means for popularizing the collection by printing out a list of titles. In this manner, patrons quickly know what books are available without searching through the entire CLSI system. Arrangement of such lists may be by call number or by author's last name. Production is simple; titles are typed into the database, which prompts the inputter for all fields, in any order desired. Once compiled, the list is sorted and standardized punctuation is added automatically. The completed bibliography is saved to disk, printed out, and photocopied for distribution. This process eliminates creation of the list manually and makes updating data or adding new entries easy to accomplish.

Significant Problems: While the software is adaptable and useful for many types of bibliographies, the capacity for storage was less than

required. A call to the vendor, however, solved the problem.

Reference: None available

Project Date(s): Fall 1987–Present

Cost: Per capita state grant money

Self-Rating: 8

Name: **Motivating Reading with Bibliographies on a Macintosh; Annotated Bibliography of Folk and Fairy Tales
and Mythology**

Library: Conrad Sulzer Regional Library (Chicago Public Library)

Contact Person: Marvin Garber

Address/Phone: 4455 N. Lincoln Ave., Chicago, IL 60625; (312) 728-8652

Profile: A major regional library serving the North Side of Chicago, with some 200,000 volumes, including special collections of local history.

Hardware: Apple IIe (not enhanced), Applied Engineering Z-87 card
(for CP/M), Applied Engineering RAMWorks II card for
memory expansion with 768K installed (used as
RAMdrive), Sider 10-megabyte hard drive, B-Sider tape
backup unit, Imagewriter II printer.

Software: *dBase II* (Ashton-Tate), chosen because of staff experience
writing programs in *dBase* programming language, allow-
ing full control over printed results and generation of
indexes.

Description: A bibliography of approximately 320 titles about
"folktales, fairy tales, and mythology in the Sulzer
Regional Library's Children's Collection," was produced
to accompany twenty-one programs entitled, as a group,
"The Year of the New Reader: Motivating Reading
through Traditional Oral Storytelling." The product,
essentially a book, totaled seventy-three pages and contained an introduction, cross-references by geographic
region, annotated bibliography, and separate indexes
(author/title) for mythology of Central, North and South
America, the West Indies, the Middle East, and Europe.
Each entry in the main bibliographic section contains
author, title, annotation, reading level, call number, geographic origins, and other bibliographic data (out of print,
date of publication, etc.). The primary purpose of the program series was to attract bilingual children into the library
for storytelling.

Significant Problems: None reported

Reference: None available

Project Date(s): October 1987 to April 1988

Cost: Already available equipment used. Staff time difficult to assess. Outside data-entry cost approximately $3,000. Printing of 500 copies, approximately $1,500.

Self-Rating: 10

Name: **Bibliographies on a Macintosh**

Library: Merriam Center Library

Contact Persons: Dennis Jenks and Joyce Wilson

Address/Phone: 1313 E. 60th St., Chicago, IL 60637; (312) 947-2163

Profile: The Charles E. Merriam Library was established more than fifty years ago and serves a group of nonprofit organizations in Chicago's Hyde Park area, including the American Planning Association, American Public Works Association, students and faculty of the University of Chicago, and the general public. The collection contains more than 150,000 monographs, reports, periodicals, and annual and irregular serials.

Hardware: Two Macintosh SEs with a combined hard-disk-drive storage of 60-megabytes, LaserWriter Plus printer. One Macintosh is equipped with an Apple PC 5.25-inch card and drives.

Software: *Microsoft Word 3.01* (Microsoft), chosen because of its flexibility. *Microsoft File 1.05* (Microsoft) was chosen because of familiarity. The software is highly recommended by the project participants.

Description: Significant problems creating bibliographies with traditional typewriters led to the use of the Macintosh. The need to retype a whole page when only a single word was out of place, underlining of titles that made ascenders and descenders difficult to read, etc., made for an unpolished product. The new Macintosh-generated format is professional looking and easy to produce. Using the word processor *Word*, the library inputs the bibliography electronically, with the program providing automatic formatting. A copy is generated on the ImageWriter printer in 14-point Geneva, a font size that is easy to proofread. The finished copy is then reduced to normal size so that page breaks, etc., come out properly. Font changes are simple with the Macintosh. A template has also been prepared for the title page, which helps to avoid redundant work.

Significant Problems: None reported

Reference: Ullman, Charlotte. "Publishing Bibliographies with the Macintosh and *MacWrite*," *Apple Library Users Group Newsletter*, April 1987, p.47.

Project Date(s): July 1986–Present

Cost: $9,400, total cost. Obtained through contract with Council of Planning Librarians.

Self-Rating: 10

# Budgeting and Accounting: Adding It All Up

Many smaller libraries do not need the heavy-duty number-crunching provided by many accounting packages, but most can make good use of a spreadsheet and templates. A spreadsheet provides the electronic equivalent of the accountant's paper and pencil, and the template provides an already constructed framework of calculations into which a library may plug its own budget numbers. Such packages can help a library to plan a budget by answering the question, "What if?" By simply changing numbers here and there in the spreadsheet, it is possible to make the budget planning process go much faster, since the spreadsheet effects all relevant changes automatically. Templates can be found for Apple computers by looking for the appropriate citation in the list of resources in the back of this volume. Using a modern computer system to help track budget expenditures for various departments or branches is a different matter, one that is addressed by some of the projects listed below.

## Further Reading

Clark, Philip M. *Microcomputer Spreadsheet Models for Libraries.* ALA, 1985.

| | |
|---|---|
| Name: | ***dBase* for Expenditures in a University Library** |
| Library: | Duke University Law Library |
| Contact Person: | Hope Breeze |
| Address/Phone: | Durham, NC 27706; (919) 684-4138 |
| Profile: | The library has 8 professionals and 19 clerical or student assistants. It houses approximately 48,000 titles and 4,700 periodicals on subscription. |
| Hardware: | NBI System |
| Software: | *dBase II* (Ashton-Tate). The software was selected because it was already in use at Duke's law school. |
| Description: | *dBase* on a microcomputer was seen as a way to simplify the manual gathering of data on acquisitions and expenditures. In order to design the system properly, several meetings with acquisitions staff were held. Some 37 different |

codes are used to categorize ordered materials. In addition, 12 geographic codes may also be assigned to the type codes. This results in 277 possible combinations and, hence, a time-consuming job. Using *dBase* the library set up three permanent, separate files (YEAR, PURGE, and ACQ), all with the same structure. YEAR cumulates weekly totals, while PURGE replaces the YEAR file when it is no longer needed. ACQ contains no data but is a template for establishing a structure for each new weekly file. The *dBase* programs that were created for this project are all relatively short but still require some understanding of a command language and enough time to program and debug the system. (The exact command files are reprinted in the citation below.) Since *dBase II* is no longer available, it is only useful for libraries that already own the program or those that wish to invest in a newer version of *dBase*. The program is used weekly by library assistants, and operation is simple.

**Significant Problems:** Entering and editing records from the menu is a useful improvement that has not yet been implemented. For now, staff uses commands that are part of the *dBase* command structure.

**Reference:** Breeze, Hope. "Totaling and Categorizing Expenditures Using *dBase*," *Library Software Review*, April 1987, p.68.

**Project Date(s):** Fall 1985–Present

**Cost:** Equipment already available. No additional expense.

**Name:** **Budget Preparation Using Spreadsheets**

**Library:** Stockton–San Joaquin County Public Library

**Contact Person:** Donna Brown

**Address/Phone:** 605 N. El Dorado St.; (209) 944-8365

**Profile:** Serves a population of over 343,000 people, with an annual circulation of over 1,177,000. Professional staff, 27; clerical, 73. Seven branch libraries and one bookmobile.

**Hardware:** DEC Rainbow 100

**Software:** *SuperCalc2* (Sorcim) was already available and capable of performing necessary budgetary tasks.

**Description:** In 1910 the County of San Joaquin began contracting with the city of Stockton for library service. Since then, different methods were devised for calculating how governmental units (branches) should pay for service, based on population and usage. Because of funding shortages (due in part to Proposition 13), it became necessary to know more precisely how much it costs to operate the branch libraries.

Because of centralized services involving cataloging, administration, supplies, etc., it became necessary to devise a set of complicated formulas, the computation of which took a great deal of staff time. Hence, a more efficient method of calculation was sought. Since an integrated online circulation system using DEC Rainbows for backup was being installed, it was logical to also use it for compilation of the budgetary data. The already-devised formulas were entered into the computer, with a separate spreadsheet for each activity. ("This assigned the amount of each budget line item to branches or activities.") Centralized services were calculated using a second set of spreadsheets, and a cost was assigned to each branch. A final spreadsheet compiled "costs for each outlet, plus centralized costs and a division of costs between city and county based on usage."

Soon after, electronic spreadsheets were used to calculate employee salaries and benefits as well as the library's preliminary budget to be submitted to the city manager. In 1986–87, the library purchased an IBM with hard disk and transferred to it the branch calculations, making it possible to do the entire operation on one large, integrated spreadsheet.

Significant Problems: None

Reference: None available

Project Date(s): 1982–Present

Cost: Since hardware and software were already available, there was no major cost to the library.

Self-Rating: 9

Name: **Automating the Book Budget**

Library: Arlington Heights Memorial Library

Contact Person: Ruth Griffith

Address/Phone: 500 N. Dunton, Arlington Heights, IL 60004; (312) 392-0100

Profile: Serves a community of approximately 66,000, with over 341,000 volumes and a staff of 39.

Hardware: Apple IIe (originally); replaced with IIgs.

Software: *VisiCalc* (VisiCorp) was originally selected, since it was one of the few spreadsheets available at the time; records later transferred to *AppleWorks* (Apple Computers) because of ease of use and interface with other modules (word processing and database management).

Description: Since the regular budgeting process did not keep track of different format categories, a computerized spreadsheet was employed to keep track of amounts spent, amounts remaining, and amounts in each category (e.g., videotapes, books, tapes, filmstrips, etc.). Such a project requires only the simplest use of a spreadsheet. Figures are tallied monthly, providing a much better way for staff to plan and allocate remaining budget amounts. The "template," or copy, of last month's figures can be saved to disk and then called up when the new month arrives, new figures are added, and a new grand total is produced, all within a fraction of the time that a manual system would require.

Significant Problems: None reported

Reference: None available

Project Date(s): 1983–Present

Cost: Hardware ($2,000) was purchased with regular annual equipment budget. Software cost, $300.

Self-Rating: Not given

# Bulletin Boards: Reaching Out to the World

The electronic bulletin board system (BBS) has made its impact on the library community in two ways: as a public access information center and as an interlibrary loan tool. A few BBSs have expanded their reach to include additional functions, e.g., as a "front-end" to an online catalog, or even providing answers to reference questions online. Still, the main thrust is the same—a locally produced database.

Simply put, a BBS is an online interactive database that may have any number of components. These usually include: electronic mail between users, upload/download of public domain software, conference areas (messages posted publicly and grouped into topical categories), and online news and articles about subjects pertaining to the theme of the BBS. Boards vary considerably in what they offer callers. Patrons calling a BBS may need to obtain a password, then wait several days before receiving final validation (i.e., full access to all board privileges). At that point, a caller can contribute to any of the conference areas, send electronic mail, and participate in other ways. They may also upload public domain software to the BBS or upload articles about relevant topics. Some boards are "read-only," permitting no input from callers. In the case of the library public access BBS, it may include online news and information about the library or the community, or it may encourage participation by involving patrons in "storyboards," message boards, and other communications. All of this, of course, is dependent upon how the library views the service and how it wishes to structure it. News about the library BBS is generally positive, though there is always the complaint about the "hacker" or system crasher who is just out to cause trouble. Most boards have ignored these callers or have built in strict security measures (see account of Lincolnet, below, for example of way to deal with problem callers).

ILL use of the BBS may have begun in Wisconsin through the innovation of Cathy Moore of the Wisconsin Interlibrary Services. Some of her adventures are chronicled below, but others may be found in articles cited in *Library Journal*, among other places, as well as in Moore's new book, *Bulletin Boards for Libraries* (Oryx, 1988).

| | |
|---|---|
| Name: | **North–Pulaski BBS** |
| Library: | Chicago Public Library |
| Contact Person: | Patrick R. Dewey |
| Address/Phone: | c/o Maywood Public Library, 12 S. Fifth Ave., Maywood, IL 60153; (312) 343-1847 |
| Profile: | North–Pulaski is a large storefront branch of the Chicago Public Library and serves a community of predominantly Hispanic patrons. It occupies approximately 6,000 square feet and is situated along North Avenue in the North–Pulaski business district. |
| Hardware: | Apple II+, two disk drives, Epson printer, 300-baud Hayes modem. |
| Software: | *ABBS* (no longer available); *PMS—People's Message System* (Bill Blue, Marilla Corp.). |
| Description: | This was the first BBS set up in a public library for public access. It was, in effect, a testing ground for this type of service in libraries. Described succinctly, and for purposes of this project, a BBS is a local online system that is interactive and available to callers who own a microcomputer with modem (or any equipment that will interact online). The North–Pulaski BBS was seen as a way to publicize library events, disseminate general information about the library, and provide a good public image for the library by making it a part of the growing online community. The North–Pulaski BBS was a public access BBS, as opposed to an ILL or library BBS, which are for professional use only. The board went through several changes and modifications as it evolved through the five years that it was online. The first of these involved software. Earlier software such as *ABBS* (Apple Bulletin Board System) had few of the modern features such as multiple boards or private electronic mail; even more frustrating, *ABBS* was prone to more frequent "crashes" than systems now offered. The *People's Message System* offered crash resistance and other features, but it would not operate at more than 300 baud, which eventually proved a problem. *PMS* did, however, provide an area in which articles could be posted, and proved convenient because it would automatically assign passwords. This system was in place for four years and proved a reliable workhorse. When the board was finally taken offline because of a lack of staff time, it had logged over 30,000 calls. Some features of this early board were several dozen articles about library service. Followers of the board (including in their numbers handicapped individuals) had carried on an active dialogue |

about philosophy of library service, computers, and life in general. One caller regularly phoned in an online "Soap Opera Digest." The system was so successful that it was highlighted in an article in *Esquire*. One fact that did not escape anyone's attention was that while *PMS* was a much better program than the one used earlier, during the three years of use, BBS software had improved incredibly. The increasing number of bulletin boards online and the people becoming involved with them apparently created a sizable market for such products.

Significant Problems: Despite hacker problems from time to time, nothing significant ever developed. Online volunteers are difficult to handle, since they are often hackers with modems just trying to set up their own "clubhouse." The lesson? Exercise extreme caution when taking in outsiders.

Reference: Dewey, Patrick. "Dear ABBS: Maintenance, Management, and Problems," *Small Computers in Libraries*, April 1982, p.1.
Dewey, Patrick. "The Electronic Bulletin Board Arrives at the Public Library," *Library Hi Tech*, Spring 1984, p.13.
Dewey, Patrick. "Library Use of Electronic Bulletin Board Systems," *Library Software Review*, Nov.–Dec. 1985, p.351.

Project Date(s): 1981–86

Cost: A grant from the Friends of the Chicago Public Library for approximately $4,300 was acquired to set up the Personal Computer Center. The same equipment was used during the evening hours to run the BBS.

Self-Rating: 10

Name: **Wellspring BBS**

Library: University of California–Irvine Biomedical Library

Contact Person: Steve Clancy

Address/Phone: Box 19556, Irvine, CA 92713; (714) 856-7309 or (714) 856-6654 (voice); (714) 856-7996 (data)

Profile: The Biomedical Library has a staff of 10 professionals and 13 clerical, serving the UCI faculty, students, staff in medicine and biological sciences, physicians, health practitioners and general public. Approximately 167,000 volumes.

Hardware: (Initially) IBM PC XT, 256K, 10-megabyte hard drive, monochrome monitor, Hayes 1200B modem, Epson FX80+ printer. Upgrades included: 1.28-megabyte RAM (AST expansion card), NEC V20 replacement for 8088 processor chip, 30-megabyte fixed disk, U.S. Robotics Courier HST modem (300–9600 baud).

Software: Began with *RBBS-PC CPC12.1A* (Capital PC Users Group), then upgraded to *CPC16.1A* (as of May 1988).

Description: Project began as a way to promote library services and resources, to publicize the library's involvement with microcomputer technology, and to experiment with microcomputer communications. Once users have logged onto the BBS, they have access to a wide variety of services, including discussion areas, electronic mail, MEDLINE, public domain software, and a "reference desk," where questions may be left for the library staff. The system went online October 4, 1985. As of February 29, 1988, Wellspring had received nearly 25,000 calls from a user base exceeding 1,400 people. Some 1,000 calls per month are received. Most of the services are medical related, including many bulletins about library hours, information, articles about topics such as AIDS and other diseases, and more general, computer-related material. The Wellspring operator spends approximately one hour per day involved in the activities of the BBS. More than 20 megabytes of public domain and shareware software are arranged in 20 different categories, including utility programs, BBS lists and ads, music programs, educational programs and tutorials, database and file management, word processing, and more. The BBS has slowly become an extension of the Biomedical Library services. Operation is 5 p.m. to 8 a.m. weekdays and 24 hours on weekends.

Significant Problems: Though considered a minor problem, each upgrade of the software has brought with it new bugs that need to be ironed out.

Reference: None available

Project Date(s): May 1985–Present

Cost: Software costs only $3; hardware cost not applicable since it is used for other purposes as well.

Self-Rating: 10

Name: **Lincolnet BBS**

Library: Maywood Public Library and the Suburban Library System

Contact Person: Patrick R. Dewey

Address/Phone: 121 S. Fifth Ave., Maywood, IL 60153; (312) 343-1847

Profile: The Suburban Library System is a multitype system serving approximately 185 libraries west of Chicago. The Maywood Public Library is a small public library serving a community of 28,000 people.

Hardware: Apple IIe, two disk drives, two 10-megabyte Sider hard drives, Hayes 1200 baud modem, Imagewriter printer.

Software: *GBBS Pro* (Micro Data Products), is a good software package that provides for complete remote system maintenance, automatic registration and passwording of users, and a wide variety of services.

Description: Lincolnet was conceived as a publicity/promotion tool. Patrons who owned microcomputers would be able to call 24 hours a day and have online access to a database about library services. Items available include book sale lists, videotape locations in the system, a local history database, the system reference newsletter, and library joblines (from Rosary College). A multitude of other information files concerning library services is also available. Callers have access to 18 different conference areas and may participate by leaving their own comments. Topics include books, movies, and computers. More than 11,000 calls have been logged to date.

Significant Problems: The most significant problem encountered was the difficulty with ''hackers,'' youthful types who enjoy putting up graffiti and otherwise ''having fun'' with the BBS. Several efforts were made to dissuade them from doing this, including making the board available only to registered users. Finally, the pranksters simply got bored and left. Password mailing solves this problem by making it difficult for hackers to obtain more than one password. They must also list their correct address in order to obtain a password, something that anyone bent on outrageous activity is not prone to do. One other problem is data entry; it is very difficult to find staff time to enter large volumes of data.

Reference: None available

Project Date(s): April 1986–Present

Cost: LSCA grant. Approximately $6,000 was spent on the project.

Self-Rating: 10

Name: **Online Catalog and Bulletin Board**

Library: Texas State Law Library

Contact Person: Kay Schlueter

Address/Phone: Supreme Court Building, Box 12367, Capitol Station, Austin, TX 78711; (512) 463-1722

Profile: With holdings in excess of 100,000 volumes and 215 periodical subscriptions, the Texas State Law Library was founded in 1971. It has special U.S. document collections, with legal history a special interest.

Hardware: MS-DOS computer with 20-megabyte hard drive and modem.

Software: *FYI-MCD* (FYI, Inc.), *DoubleDOS* (SoftLogic Solutions), *Ultracard* (Small Library Computing).

Description: A text-retrieval online database (essentially an electronic bulletin board system), which allows library patrons to dial in remotely and have access to the library's card catalog, a listing of more than 1,800 titles accumulated over a two-year span. Setting up such a system involved several steps, beginning with downloading and editing RLIN records. A catalog card production system, *Ultracard*, is used to create ASCII text files (files that are universally understood by computers). The BBS software used, *FYI*, allows searching for or retrieving data in a full-text retrieval method. Truncation and Boolean searching are also permitted. The system also contains tables of contents of State Bar of Texas publications and the State Law Library's periodicals holdings. Both attorneys and librarians can search all of these databases from any remote location via a microcomputer and modem. This system goes beyond just full-text retrieval, and the library can also make use of the program's ability to handle electronic mail, chat with users, create conference boards, and the posting of "general" articles or information for users. Using *DoubleDOS*, a time-sharing program, the library can create a situation that allows a microcomputer to be used in-house by staff and accessed remotely at the same time. As of 1987 the library had nearly 2,000 records online for users.

Significant Problems: Search time is doubled with the use of the time-sharing program. The solution is to dedicate a computer to the online catalog, if possible.

Reference: Hambleton, James. "Micro-Based, Dial-Up Library Catalog," *M300 and PC Report*, Mar. 1987, p.1.

Project Date(s): Fall 1986–Present

Cost: Equipment already in place; no additional funding required.

Self-Rating: 8

# Circulation

| | |
|---:|:---|
| Name: | **Overdues on a Macintosh** |
| Library: | Markley Elementary School Library |
| Contact Person: | Sally Tweedle |
| Address/Phone: | Church Road, Malvern, PA 19355 |
| Library Profile: | Serves a public elementary school of 510 students. |
| Hardware: | Macintosh with 512K |
| Software: | *FileMaker Plus* (Nashoba Systems) |
| Description: | This library has no automated circulation system, but found that automating only one task, in this case, the writing and printing of overdue notices, was a step in the right direction. Several features of *FileMaker Plus* are exceptionally useful. The first is the "Scripts" feature, a short-hand method of moving between different components such as data entry, preview of notice, and printing. The second is the "Look-up" feature, which allows student names to be accessed in a second related file for additional information on homeroom, borrowing limitations, etc. |
| Significant Problems: | Two problems reported were the lack of wrap-around word processing (see article cited below). |
| Reference: | Tweedle, Sally. "Computerized Overdue Notices Using *FileMaker Plus* & a 512K Enhanced Macintosh. In Edward J. Valauskas, ed., *Macintoshed Libraries* (Apple Library Users Group, 1988), p.47. |
| Project Date(s): | Not given |
| Cost: | Not given |
| Self-Rating: | Not given |

| | |
|---:|:---|
| Name: | **Automated Circulation System** |
| Library: | Seminole Community College |
| Contact Person: | Thomas L. Reitz |
| Address/Phone: | 100 Weldon Blvd., Sanford, FL 32773; (407) 323-1450 x450 |

Profile: The Seminole Community College Library serves a faculty of 240 and a student body of approximately 5,400. Library contains more than 63,000 book volumes.

Hardware: Burroughs (UNISYS) B-25 expansion disk, Caere light wands, Burroughs printer, Okidata printer.

Software: Written by local contract programmer.

Description: For twenty years a manual circulation system, which relied on the hand copying of personal and bibliographic information, had been employed at the college. It became necessary to replace it with an automated system for several reasons: the copying of incorrect information, both bibliographic and personal; illegible handwriting, which made it difficult or time-consuming to send overdue reminders; the lack of counter space required to do the copying; and the difficulty of retrieving information from call slips. Some two years of planning ensued to produce a system that would reflect correct bibliographic and personal data, provide answers to the often-asked question, "What books do I have out?" and generate meaningful statistical data. For a variety of practical reasons (including local lightning problems), it was decided not to go with the college's mainframe, especially since the library felt that it would not have first priority. Instead, it went with the Burroughs B-25 ("essentially a personal computer supporting up to four additional workstations"). This system could communicate with the mainframe but could not be dependent upon it. A programmer was employed to write the original software (and maintain and modify it as required).

Significant Problems: A homemade system is not recommended by Reitz. "We have been particularly fortunate to have a supportive programmer and administration and especially supportive data center personnel. Without this support, we could have had a very difficult time."

Reference: Reitz, Thomas L. "The Seminole Community College Automated Circulation System," *Library Software Review*, Dec. 1987, p.349.

Project Date(s): Online July 1986

Cost: Funds came from the library operating budget over a two-year period. Total cost: $48,064.40. Programming costs were $15,000. Hardware costs were $25,900.45. Software and related items (e.g., data cartridges) were $7,188.70.

Self-Rating: 9

Name: **Videotape List**

Library: Maywood Public Library

Contact Person: Kristin Flanders

Address/Phone: 121 S. Fifth Ave., Maywood, IL 60153; (312) 343-1847

Profile: Maywood Public Library serves a community of approximately 28,000 residents, approximately 70 percent black, the remainder split between Hispanic and white. It has one branch library (storefront) and one main library.

Hardware: Apple IIe, two disk drives, Imagewriter II printer.

Software: *AppleWorks* database component (Apple Computers).

Description: This simple project provides a printout catalog of the videotape collection, which, though growing, currently stands at more than 800 titles. One of the problems with the collection has been that since the library has limited space, it is impossible to display all of the videotape boxes in the library, as is often the case in videotape stores. The boxes are flattened and then laminated and kept in magazine cases for browsing. The latter is only a partial solution, since many patrons do not care to browse in this manner. The microcomputer-produced catalog, easily created using the *AppleWorks* database manager, provides a listing by title. Fields for this database are: title, length (minutes), color or black and white, and a code. The code allows for sorting the database by type of film (horror or educational, for example) and producing special catalogs for specialized audiences. The main catalog is available free and is updated every few weeks. Only as many copies as needed between updates are created on the copy machine. Every six months the catalog is sent to all registered users of the videotape collection by U.S. mail to remind them of the collection and to point out the many new titles.

Significant Problems: None

Reference: None available

Project Date(s): Ongoing since mid-1986

Cost: Equipment and software already in place for other work.

Self-Rating: 10

Name: *Circulation Plus* **in a School Library**

Library: Johnson Elementary School Media Center

Contact Person: Beth Clemensen

Address/Phone: 1730 Wilkes Ave., Davenport, IA 52804

Profile: Elementary (K–6) school with approximately 6,000 items in its collection.

Hardware: Apple IIe

Software: *Circulation Plus* (Follett)

Description: This school went from manual records to a fully automated, in-house circulation system. Some specific experiences, both good and bad, are worth sharing. Start-up time for the system was approximately six months. The library has 6,000 items, with 3,500 entered by volunteer help and the rest "on the run." The Follett system is a barcode system, so records may be either entered in advance or as they are circulated (Follett also offers a whole range of extra services for an extra fee, such as sending new books with barcodes already attached, data entry, etc.). This new system has given the library more control over the collection than before. For instance, it can now be determined who has what materials outstanding quickly. (Overdues, it is reported, fell by 50 percent!) Reserves also increased significantly, since it was now possible to note reserve status when the book was checked in or out. (The most spectacular effect is the report that these new automated procedures doubled circulation!) A monthly report for the staff and others is generated in a few minutes.

Significant Problems:  The staff at the school makes the following suggestions: become familiar with the demo disk, though keep in mind it is only a sales sample; read the manual carefully; talk with other librarians who have already installed the system and attempt to spend at least four hours working with it in advance.

Reference:  Clemensen, Beth. "One School on Circ. Plus," *Apple Library Users Group Newsletter*, Oct. 1987, p.53.

Project Date(s):  Spring 1986

Cost:  Not given

Self-Rating:  Not given

Name:  **Software Lending**

Library:  Liverpool Public Library

Contact Person:  Jean Armour Polly

Address/Phone:  Tulip and Second Sts., Liverpool, NY 13088; (315) 457-0310

Profile:  Serves a population of just over 50,000. Annual circulation is over 330,000, and the library owns approximately 54,000 titles.

Hardware:  Apple IIe, 128K, Atari 1040ST, with one megabyte and 720 RAM, RGB color monitor, mouse, shared dot-matrix printer (also this system has a Casio CZ-230S synthesizer, TEAC dual stereo cassette deck); Panasonic Business Partner (IBM compatible), 640K dual floppy drives, Macintosh Plus (2) with one megabyte RAM, and internal 800K microfloppy disk drives, external 800K micro-floppy disk drive, mouse. Apple IIgs, with one-megabyte RAM, RGB color monitor, 2 800K microfloppy disk drives, 5 1/4-inch floppy disk drive, ImageWriter II dot-matrix printer with color capability, CP/M card, mouse. Apple LaserWriter Plus laser printer available. Many of the microcomputers are "Appletalked" (networked together to take advantage of different peripherals, such as the LaserWriter printer). A CD-ROM drive is projected for the next year.

Software: The selection of software for this project includes packages for all age groups, including approximately equal proportions for educational, recreational, and utility functions.

Description: The library circulates word-processing packages, database management systems, and spreadsheets. Remarkably, they have been circulating materials since 1984, currently averaging about 10,000 items per year. The original idea called for parents and others to select software for use that would perhaps only maintain a child's or adult's interest for a short time, thereby saving on the expense of a costly package. The first step was a community survey to determine which computers people owned.

Significant Problems: Originally, only software for computers the library owned was circulated (Apple). When software was finally purchased for other computers, a problem arose when a patron returned something that was apparently not working and there was no way to inspect it. The library now owns computers for all software it circulates. An effort is made to create a backup (archival) copy of all software, but this takes time and is not always possible. One thing that helps a lot is to write-protect as many disks as possible. Approximately 5 percent of the collection is sitting on the "dead" shelf awaiting replacement. IBM (MS and PC-DOS) software is much easier for patrons to ruin than other types.

Reference: For a comprehensive look at what types of software libraries collect for public use, see Jean Armour Polly's *Essential Guide to Apple Computers in Libraries, Volume 1: Public Technology: The Library Public Access Computer* (Meckler, 1986). In it, she presents the results of her survey of some seventy libraries.

Project Date(s): April 1, 1984–Present

Cost: The library is currently spending about $13,000 per year for staff and public software.

Self-Rating: 10

Name: **Corporate Library Circulation System**

Library: General Foods USA, Technical Information Center

Contact Person: Nancy J. Mandeville

Address/Phone: 555 S. Broadway, Tarrytown, NY 10591; (914) 335-6185

Profile: This special library was founded in 1939 and contains some 10,000 titles with special focus on biochemistry, chemistry, engineering, food science, and nutrition.

Hardware: IBM PC, 10-megabyte hard disk, Epson FX-185 printer.

Software: *dBase III* (Ashton-Tate; recommended by computer applications department and used by others in company); *Quickindex* (Fox and Geller).

Description: This research library has more than 3,000 books in circulation. Manual circulation methods were no longer considered feasible and consumed too much staff time, so computerization was considered the only viable alternative. Another benefit was the ability to reduce book loss (through greater control) and to generate overdue notices. The details of what the system would do were specified by the library staff. Since the project was performed internally, programming staff familiar with *dBase* were able to perform all of the programming and debugging as required. The system as completed was intended to be an interim system until a true online catalog system could be obtained. Approximately twenty-five pages of *dBase* codes were written to provide a menu-driven system. The main menu has selections of "Check Out," "Return/Edit," "Search the Database," "Print Reports," and "Pack and Re-Index the Database." Other options exist within each section as submenus. For example, the database "Search" function permits searching by accession number, call number, title, and author. Reports can be generated and sorted by author, title, or call number. First and second overdue notices, based on when a book is first checked out, are generated weekly. Reports include a borrower's current loans (useful for when people transfer or leave the company). Six months were required to specify, program, write the manual, train the staff, and debug the system. Some of the initial benefits have been that information need only be typed once (and may then be sorted many ways) and reports that are more accurate and up-to-date.

Significant Problems: It is highly recommended that this type of major project be initiated only by someone with advanced *dBase* programming skills.

Reference: Mandeville, Nancy J. "Developing a Corporate Library Circulation System Using *dBase III*," *Library Software Review*, Nov.–Dec. 1987, p.370.

Project Date(s): 1985

Cost: Since project was developed internally, it is difficult to assign costs except for purchase of hardware and software. The computer was approximately $3,500, the software approximately $700.

Self-rating: 9

Name: **Special Library Circulation File; Routing Periodicals**

Library: Merriam Center Library

Contact Person: Michael A. Wilson

Address/Phone: 1313 E. 60th St., Chicago, IL 60637; (312) 947-2162

Profile: The Charles E. Merriam Library was formed over 50 years ago and serves a group of nonprofit organizations in Chicago's Hyde Park area, including the American Planning Association, American Public Works Association, students and faculty of the University of Chicago, and the general public. The collection contains over 50,000 monographs, 100,000 reports, 800 periodical titles, and 1,000 annual and irregular serials.

Hardware: Macintosh SE, 20-megabyte internal hard drive.

Software: *Microsoft File*, Version 1.05 (Microsoft), because of staff familiarity. Circulation or routing template is available through the Apple Library Template Exchange.

Description: The purpose of this project was to automate a circulation system previously maintained in a paper file. The paper system was a magazine routing system for researchers and patrons who wanted to charge out periodicals for office use. The main problem involved 65 researchers wishing to have a variety of periodicals with differing publication frequencies. This posed a great problem in manual record-keeping. Using *Microsoft File*, an effort was made to match the original 3-by-5-inch card matrix. The result was a circulation template with fields enough to cover all possible combinations. This not only eliminates the manual paper system but produces a file that can be searched as well.

Significant Problems: None reported

Reference: Wilson, Michael A. "Using the Macintosh to Create a Circulation File for a Special Library," in *The Macintoshed Library* (Apple Library Users Group, 1987), p.12–14.

Project Date(s): Spring and Summer 1987

Cost: Library operating budget. Total cost: $2,500.

Self-Rating: 8

| Name: | **Videocassette Control** |
|---|---|
| Library: | Grace A. Dow Memorial Library |
| Contact Person: | Randy Dykhuis |
| Address/Phone: | 60 Library Plaza N.E., Grand Rapids, MI 49503; (616) 456-3601 |
| Profile: | This library has an annual circulation of over 600,000 in a community of approximately 67,000. Holdings are approximately 192,000 volumes. |
| Hardware: | IBM PC XT, 640K RAM, two disk drives. |
| Software: | *dBase III+* (Ashton-Tate) was selected because of its relational capabilities, large capacity, and popularity. |
| Description: | The explosion of videocassette tape rentals at libraries in recent years has led to many problems, including insufficient methods of control. Grace A. Dow Memorial Library began the automation of its video collection with *AppleWorks* and an Apple computer, but the system, while producing a catalog of titles, had other problems that made it impractical. The major difficulties were overcoming the use of four floppy disks (a cumbersome procedure), an inability to sort the records (they were using the word processor in *AppleWorks*), and cataloging and processing that was still done manually (including shelflist cards that were still typed on a typewriter). What the staff needed was a better way to enter titles, print cards, print monthly updates, and permit subject access. With the use of *dBase III+* it was possible to write a menu-driven program for a videocassette system. Although this required a great deal of additional time learning and writing program code in the *dBase* command language, it finally yielded a menu-driven program that performs most of the required tasks. Main menu choices are (1) add new videocassette title; (2) print (shelflist cards, catalog, updates); (3) edit/delete records; (4) display records; (5) exit. The program was written entirely by the reference librarian, Randy Dykhuis, and is actually a group of 24 smaller programs that work together. Since the program is menu-driven, it requires little staff training, and paraprofessionals and clerical staff may do the data entry. |
| Significant Problems: | Programming in *dBase* turned into a major problem, requiring work on and off for a year. Anyone attempting duplication of this project should be well versed in programming or have access to someone who is prepared to do the work. In fact, calls to the vendor were necessary in order to remedy certain programming difficulties, and even the vendor did not always have an immediate answer. |

Reference:  *Library Software Review*, Aug. 1987, p.190.

Project Date(s):  Not given

Cost:  Software costs were about $400 (mail order); hardware was already in place.

Self-rating:  7

Name:  **Automated Circulation System**

Library:  Lucy Hill Patterson Memorial Library

Contact Person:  Jerry Wickwire

Address/Phone:  201 Ackerman St., Rockdale, TX 76567

Profile:  Small library with an annual circulation of over 20,000 in a community of approximately 11,000 people.

Hardware:  Apple IIe, Profile hard disk drive.

Software:  *PFS:FILE* (Software Publishing), *Circulation Plus* (Follett).

Description:  After installation of an automated catalog-card production system and a computerized order file, the decision was made to automate circulation. The library contracted out to enter approximately 500 books per week onto batch diskettes for transfer into the hard disk drive. Eventually, the collection was barcoded and activated after approximately 80 percent of the collection had been processed. Finished system allows library access to more patron information (overdues, etc.) and a faster method for tracking materials.

Significant Problems:  Barcoding took longer than anticipated, but solution of "finishing-on-the-fly" solved the problem.

Reference:  Wickwire, Jerry. "Library Automation—How We Did It," *Apple Library Users Group Newsletter*, July 1987, p.47.

Project Date(s):  Total automation project took approximately four years, exact dates unknown.

Cost:  Not given

Self-Rating:  Not given

Name:  **AppleWorks Circulation System**

Library:  Danville Area Senior High School

Contact Person:  John A. Nied

Address/Phone:  Northumberland St., Danville, PA 17821; (717) 275-1281

Profile:  12,000 volumes. Serves grades 9–12.

Hardware:  Apple IIe with RAMworks 1024 card.

Software:  *AppleWorks* (Apple Computers) since it was already available and librarian knew how to use it.

Description:  This unusual project used *AppleWorks* as a total library circulation system. Using the database management component, the library set up simple records to track materials on loan to students. If there was sufficient memory for storage, as many records as required could be maintained. Records or reports can be sorted and created by any field, including by homeroom, teacher, or book, or a total listing of all overdues can be produced (as can a listing by student name). The big advantage of using this program is its ease of start-up and use. Still, for all its advantages, the Danville Area School District is looking to a specialized circulation system for the future and sees *AppleWorks* as a stopgap measure.

Significant Problems: Such a project should have more than a 128K Apple. Staff should not do inputting of data, initially, if at all possible.

Reference: *Apple Library Users Group Newsletter*, Spring 1987, p.42.

Project Date(s): 1986–Present

Cost: Not given

Self-Rating: 8.9

Name: **Software Lending**

Library: Kansas State University

Contact Person: R. S. Talab

Address/Phone: 224 Bluemont Hall, Kansas State University, Manhattan, KS 66506

Profile: The university has an enrollment of more than 18,000 and a faculty of 2,215. The total book collection exceeds 900,000 volumes, with 8,000 periodical subscriptions.

Hardware: The laboratory owns twenty Apple II enhanced computers, eight Macintosh computers, and eight Apple IIgs.

Software: For maintenance and circulation chores *Circ/Cat* (Winnebago) system, and approximately 300 software packages that support the College of Education's curriculum.

Description: In fact, two projects in one: circulating software, and automating the circulation of software in a computer learning lab. The automation project was selected in order to better control software that was on loan, reserve, etc., and because cataloging of the collection could be directly keyed into the program. Winnebago's *Circ/Cat* met both of these needs. Software is checked out using a student ID (with barcode). Only doctoral students and faculty may check materials out for home or office (master's students may do so if they have a note from faculty). Returned software is run on computer to check for defects. If an item is not returned, it is charged against the student's main library account. Archival copies of software and documentation are created by staff and kept in separate three-ring binders. One copy is stored. Copyright notices are posted in the area to alert patrons against illegal copying.

The computer system has improved the whole operation in numerous ways, including making more software available and increasing the amount of donated software.

Significant Problems: Suggestions for avoiding problems include faculty involvement from the beginning planning stages. Faculty members need to be convinced of the need for such a system (e.g., greater inventory control). Another problem involves trying to determine whether or not a software package has been damaged by running it upon return, not always an easy task.

Reference: *Small Computers in Libraries,* Mar.1987.

Project Date(s): 1984; 1988; ongoing

Cost: The circulation system (*Circ/Cat*), binders, vinyl pages, photocopying, disks, computers, bar wands, and related items totaled about $8,000 (circulating software was purchased separately and information about its cost was not returned in the survey). Replacement and other purchases run about $1,000 to $1,500 annually.

Self-Rating: Not given

# Desktop Publishing
# and Graphics

Desktop publishing has become the most popular area of microcomputing in recent years. With the aid of a micro and appropriate software, the user can create a finished product that will rival anything produced by the local layout artist or typesetter. Entry is not cheap; it still requires a desktop publishing package, a good printer (preferably a laser), not to mention the computer itself. The advantages for libraries are obvious. Using electronic clip art, elaborate fonts, borders, layout techniques, etc., the traditional library flier, newsletter, or sign can be a dazzling product produced at a fraction of the cost and in a fraction of the time (no longer is it necessary to wait for the printer to finish since a high-speed photocopier or laser printer will do just as well).

|  |  |
|---:|:---|
| Name: | **Creating Fliers on a Macintosh** |
| Library: | Lincoln High School |
| Contact Person: | Anitra Gordon |
| Address/Phone: | 7425 Willis Rd., Ypsilanti, MI 48197; (313) 484-7020 |
| Profile: | Not given |
| Hardware: | Macintosh, laser printer |
| Software: | *MacWrite* (Apple Computers), *MacPaint* (Apple Computers), *ClickArt Publications* (T/Maker). |
| Description: | Three-fold fliers were developed by library staff to introduce teachers to a wide variety of services offered beyond books. The fliers are "flashy," deliberately so to attract the teacher who has been "jaded by years of traditional notices." The material included in the fliers was relatively straightforward, including the nature of the collection, technical processes, collection management, and some ideas about what it takes to run a library. The basic philosophy of library service—and a request for help in retrieving overdue items and getting students to sign up for library cards—was also included. After deciding upon the message for a flier, each page was created on the Mac using *MacWrite*, *MacPaint*, and clip art. Graphics that |

were used included a computer, book shelf, and a clipboard. A laser printer was used and the printouts taped to a backing sheet, photocopied with a high-quality printer and copies produced on tulip-red paper in order to avoid bleeding from one side to the other.

Significant Problems: None reported.

Reference: Gordon, Anitra. ''Fashionable Fliers Introduce Macintosh and a Laser Printer,'' *Apple Library Users Group Newsletter*, Jan. 1988, p.65.

Project Date(s): September 1987

Cost: Regular library budget. Materials taken to copy stores for photocopying.

Self-Rating: 9

Name: **Poster Production**

Library: Maywood Public Library

Contact Person: Kristin Flanders

Address/Phone: 121 S. Fifth Ave., Maywood, IL 60153; (312) 343-1847

Profile: Maywood Public Library serves a community of approximately 28,000 residents, approximately 70 percent black, the remainder split between Hispanic and white. It has one branch library (storefront) and one main library.

Hardware: Apple IIe, Imagewriter II printer.

Software: *The Print Shop* (Broderbund) and various other graphic packages.

Description: Before the advent of the microcomputer, the Maywood library staff had to laboriously prepare by hand any fliers, posters, or other graphics materials to advertise services or products. Now many staff members, including pages, can produce handsome posters to boost circulation, library classes, special collections of new books, speakers, National Library Week, summer reading programs, etc. *The Print Shop*, the major program used, makes it simple to design a poster by merely following menus. Words, pictures (from the program's own supply), and borders are designated, and in just minutes a new creation comes streaming out of the printer. Most popular are the banners used for book sales (and sometimes for staff birthdays!).

Significant Problems: A constant supply of fresh ribbons (or a re-inker) is required in order to do a lot of graphics.

Reference: None available

Project Date(s): 1985–Present

Cost: State per capita grant.

Self-rating: 10

Name: **Library Tour Using *HyperCard***

Library: Apple Computers, Inc.

Contact Person: Monica Ertel

Address/Phone: 10380 Bandley Dr., Mail Stop SC, Apple Library, Cupertino, CA 95014; (408) 973-2552

Profile: This special library, with approximately 1,000 book titles and 400 periodical subscriptions, serves the Apple Computer Corporation. Special interests are personal computers, microcomputers, engineering, and marketing. The library features a Software Resource Center.

Hardware: Macintosh Plus, Macintosh SE, Macintosh II.

Software: *HyperCard* (Apple Computers) because of its visual interface, ease of use, and its applicability in libraries.

Description: The age-old problem of showing patrons how to use the library has been tackled by the new technology. Macintosh *HyperCard*, software that produces "stacks" of cards, was used to simulate a tour of the library. Both materials and services are highlighted in this visually appealing display. The Apple library employed a graphic designer as a consultant, but anyone can produce a similar tour on the Mac ("a good eye for design is essential"). Training or practice in designing with *HyperCard* is vital, but once done, the finished product is easy to use. The Macintosh sits near the front of the library with a sign that says "Library Tour," and patrons go through the facility at their own pace, receiving an introduction to the library without staff intervention. Such a tour may be as detailed as the staff wishes to make it, including digitized pictures of the library, graphic representations of certain areas (card catalogs, stacks, etc.). By using the "connectivity" of *HyperCard*, users may customize the tour. Design can be worked out with a diagram or schematic prior to actual creation of the stacks.

Significant Problems: None

Reference: None available

Project Date(s): 1987–Present

Cost: Regular library operating budget.

Self-Rating: 9

Name: **Newsletter and Calendar Production**

Library: Brighton High School

Contact Person: Bill Groomer

Address/Phone: 2220 E. Bengal Blvd., Salt Lake City, UT 84070; (801) 565-7562

Profile: Library serves 2,200 students with 16,000 volumes.

Hardware: Macintosh, LaserWriter printer

Software: *Microsoft Word* (Microsoft), *PageMaker* (Aldus), *CalendarMaker* (CE Software), *Art Roundup* (Dubl-Click Software).

Description: This high school library has shown that the Mac and a variety of software can be used to create useful and attractive newsletters and calendars of events for distribution to patrons. Using *Microsoft Word* (a word processor), text is generated and then used with *PageMaker* (a desktop publishing package) to create calendars. To enhance these, a package called *Art Roundup* is used to "flip, rotate, and edit graphics" beyond the capabilities of the other packages. With these programs the library can prepare its own camera-ready copy. The calendar of events is created separately using an inexpensive program called *Calendar-Maker*. Basic calendars can be created entirely within this program, but more sophisticated, polished work can be enhanced by "importing" the basic calendar into *MacDraw* (Apple Computers) or *PageMaker*. *CalendarMaker* allows for the creation of "pictorial calendars," "full page calendars," and "two month calendars," all menu choices. It is also suggested that *Art Roundup*, a desktop accessory, be considered as an efficient source for bringing artwork into the calendar.

Significant Problems: None reported

Reference: Groomer, Bill. "New Calendars for the New Year," *Apple Library Users Group Newsletter*, Jan. 1988, p.49.

Project Date(s): 1987–Present

Cost: Not given

Self-Rating: Not given

Name: **Desk Schedules**

Library: Evanston Public Library

Contact Person: Charles Anderson

Address/Phone: 1703 Orrington Ave., Evanston, IL 60201; (312) 866-0315

Profile: Serves a population of over 70,000 with 178,000 titles (333,390 volumes), with an annual circulation in excess of 800,000. Special interests include art, with special collections in antique silver (Berg Collection), and music (Sadie Coe Collection).

Hardware: Compaq Deskpro 286

Software: *Lotus 1-2-3* (Lotus Development Corp.), which was already owned by library. Additional programs included *Sideways* (Funk Software) and *Prokey* (RoseSoft), which were helpful but not essential.

Description: Even desk schedules are now automated at some libraries, making erasing and changing paper schedules unnecessary. This project was simple enough; a program using *Lotus 1-2-3* was used to create a template (a blank form that can be used over and over). This form has the names of staff and weekly desk schedules assigned to macros (automatic typing) that load into the spreadsheet. The person supervising or creating the schedule fills in the new information and prints out a copy. Staff time required is approximately thirty minutes.

Significant Problems: Keep this type of project simple to make it effective.

Reference: Anderson, Charles. "Desk Schedules—The Easy Way," *Wilson Library Bulletin*, June 1987, p.55.

Project Date(s): 1986–87.

Cost: None, except thirty minutes of staff time.

Self-Rating: 10

Name: **Computerized Typesetting**

Library: Kansas State Library

Contact Person: James Carroll

Address/Phone: Kansas State Library, State Capital, Third Floor, Topeka, KS 66612

Profile: A staff of twenty-four maintains a collection of some 53,000 volumes, serving a population of 2.3 million.

Hardware: IBM PC or compatible

Software: *dBase III* (Ashton-Tate)

Description: The computer was used to speed production of a guide to the manuscripts of North Dakota Institute for Regional Studies. Using *dBase III*, the material was entered into a file, edited, and formatted for printing. This file would contain embedded printer codes and would be sent directly to a local printer for typesetting. A database was set up with fields supporting main entry, title, date and physical description, biographical notes, scope and contents, donor, finding aids, notes, and the collection number of the institute. AACR2 format was followed. Student workers were hired to do the inputting of data.

Significant Problems: It was discovered that the memo field of *dBase* does not allow formatting, which is where the scope and content field would go. Four character fields of 256 characters each were used instead.

Reference: Carroll, James. "Using *dBase III* to Prepare Material for Computerized Typesetting." *Library Software Review*, Nov.–Dec. 1987, p.371.

Project Date(s): 1984

Cost: Not given
Self-Rating: Not given

Name: **Publishing a Newsletter on a Macintosh**
Library: Merriam Center Library
Contact Person: Dennis Jenks
Address/Phone: 1313 E. 60th St., Chicago, IL 60637; (313) 947-2165
Profile: The Charles E. Merriam Library was established more than fifty years ago and serves a group of nonprofit organizations in Chicago's Hyde Park area, including the American Planning Association, American Public Works Association, students and faculty of the University of Chicago, and the general public. The collection contains more than 150,000 monographs, reports, periodicals and annual and irregular serials.
Hardware: Macintosh SE, 40-megabyte hard disk, 1200-baud modem, LaserWriter Plus (originally used 512K-enhanced Macintosh, then Macintosh Plus with 20-megabyte hard disk, LaserWriter Plus printer).
Software: *Microsoft Word* (Microsoft); originally used *MacWrite* (Apple Computers) and *MacTerminal* (Apple Computers), then *Microsoft File* (Microsoft) and *Kermit* (PC-SIG).
Description: Hoping to save money (by not using the mainframe computer) and making data entry easier, library staff are now producing *Recent Publications on Governmental Problems* using a Macintosh. Cover and news sections are done using *Word 3.0* and *MacDraw* (Apple Computers). The main body of bibliographic entries is created using the Mac program *File*. The database that results is also becoming the library's main catalog. The mainframe is not eliminated. The *MS File* is sent as a text file with *Kermit*, a telecommunications program, to an Amdahl mainframe, which then sorts and formats the text properly using a variety of programs.
Significant Problems: Documenting all procedures is a must for anyone considering this type of project.
Reference: Jenks, Dennis A. and Valauskas, Edward J. "Macintosh-Mainframe Applications in a Special Library," *Apple Library Users Group Newsletter*, Oct. 1986, p.25.
Project Date(s): Summer 1986
Cost: Library operating budget: approximately $1,600 originally; approximate additional current costs are $5,500.
Self-Rating: 8

Name: **Community Resource Directory**

Library: Conrad Sulzer Regional Library

Contact Person: Marvin Garber

Address/Phone: 4455 N. Lincoln Ave., Chicago, IL 60625; (312) 728-8652

Profile: A major regional library serving the North Side of Chicago with some 200,000 volumes, including special collections of local history.

Hardware: Apple IIe (not enhanced), Applied Engineering Z-87 card (for CP/M), Applied Engineering RAMWorks II card for memory expansion with 768K installed (used as RAMdrive), Sider 10-megabyte hard drive, B-Sider tape backup unit, Imagewriter II printer.

Software: *dBase II* (Ashton-Tate), chosen because of staff experience writing programs in *dBase* programming language, which allows full control over printed results and generation of indexes.

Description: Printed directories often have limited life spans. However, they are increasingly being created with the aid of computers, often with a desktop publisher or even a simple word processing program. These are often community resource directories that can be frequently updated. This handsome directory of community resources for the Chicagoland area was the result of this endeavor. The directory contains 98 pages of alphabetically arranged community organizations, each with address, contact, purpose of the organization, services, eligibility for services, fees (if any), meeting locations, publications (if any), and hours. A project team of five people was organized to plan the acquisition and entry of data and the finished product. The *dBase* programming project involves three distinct steps: creating the database, inputting and editing the data, and writing the procedure or *dBase* command file that will print the data in a format desired.

Significant Problems: None reported

Reference: None available

Project Date(s): June 1987 (original project)

Cost: Printing, typesetting, and graphics cost approximately $4,200. Hired labor approximately $7,200.

Self-rating: 10

Name: **Desktop Publishing: "Golden Years Directory"**

Library: Dublin (Ireland) Public Libraries

Contact Person: Mairead Mullaney

Address/Phone: Central Department, Cumberland House, Fenian St., Dublin 2, Ireland 61 90 00

Profile: An independent library authority, staffed and directed by professionals at IFLA-recommended levels.

Hardware: Amstrad PC1512 (IBM compatible) and Epson LX800 printer.

Software: *Nutshell Database* (Leading Edge), *Wordstar 1512 (MicroPro)* word-processing package, and *Fleet Street Editor Desktop Publisher* (Spectrum HoloByte). Selected because of integration capabilities.

Description: A handsome paperbound community resource directory intended for use by senior citizens. Some of the many topics included are free services, arthritis treatment, asthma, dental care, legal advice, travel, taxation, and more. An extensive index makes further investigation easy. The project originally arose out of "Active Age Week," a week for the elderly organized by local authorities in Dublin. The libraries saw their role as a provider of information and with the assistance of the Friends of the Elderly, came up with the "Guide," which proved to be so popular that it ultimately resulted in a second edition. Some 55,000 copies of the new edition have already been distributed with a reprinting possible.

Significant Problems: None reported

Reference: *Apple Library Users Group Newsletter*, Jan. 1988, p.36.

Project Date(s): September 1987–March 1988

Cost: Financial assistance from the Bank of Ireland.

Self-Rating: Not given

Name: **Retrospective Conversion on a Microcomputer**

Library: Jane Beaumont is an independent library systems consultant. Information for this project was gathered from several sources, including Jane's notes in the proceedings of the *Small Computers in Libraries* conference.

Contact Person: Jane Beaumont

Address/Phone: 111 Russell Hill Rd., Toronto, Ontario, M4V 2S9, Canada; (416) 922-9364

Profile: Not applicable

Hardware: IBM or M300

Software: See below.

Description: Instead of just telling the story of one library that survived retrospective conversion, it seems better to note what people who are involved with such projects have to say about a system or method for proceeding. Many libraries have now been through *retrospective conversion*—the process of converting a library's old records (usually a card catalog) to a machine-readable format that can be used in an automated circulation system or put to other uses. At a recent conference Beaumont, a consultant, outlined a number of steps that determined the most efficient way in which to achieve conversion, since the method involved depends heavily upon the finished product's use, e.g., circulation or cataloging, etc. Pertinent questions include:

Will the records conform to the MARC standard or some subset of that standard?

What cataloging standards are to be used—AACR2 or a mix?

What is the approach to authority control?

If a bibliographic utility is the source of records, who owns the records and what are the library's rights in reusing the records it has created?

Once a project has been decided upon, many conversion methods utilize a microcomputer as part of the process at some point. If the conversion takes place in-house, microcomputer involvement may figure in at least one of three ways: (1) using a micro with software such as Cuadra Associates' STAR system to serve as host system when "cataloging copy from a microfiche or hard copy source, editing it as required and then keying the data into the database''; (2) accessing the complete MARC database on CD-ROM using a microcomputer as an in-house online source; and (3) using an IBM or M300 to find and process records through a bibliographic utility such as OCLC, UTLAS, WLN, and RLIN (i.e., using the microcomputer as a simple terminal). A second method involves the use of a service bureau. In such cases, the service bureau takes the prepared record (done in-house) and then matches it against an established, comprehensive database. In-house staff work involves the generation of a "search key" (ISBN, ISSN, LCCN, etc.) and such other information (brief title, author, publisher, date) as required to ascertain the match. Once correctly matched, the library has a complete record for its database.

A third way to proceed is to have the service bureau do the entire job, working from the library shelflist.

Significant Problems: Not available
Reference: None available
Project Date(s): None available
Funding Source: None available
Self-Rating: None available

# Government Documents Control

| | |
|---|---|
| Name: | **Government Documents and Micros** |
| Library: | Richter Library, University of Miami |
| Contact Person: | Tony Harvell |
| Address/Phone: | Box 248214, Coral Gables, FL 33124; (305) 284-3155 |
| Profile: | Provides library services to over 11,000 students and 1,200 faculty. Holdings include over 1,400,000 volumes. A staff of more than 200 includes some 50 professionals. |
| Hardware: | M300 (IBM PC) |
| Software: | In-house development |
| Description: | This project represents a cluster of successfully completed activities in the Government Documents Department of the University of Miami. Included were circulation, indexing, union list creation, word processing, spreadsheets, file management, and government-produced, machine-readable data files. Many of these projects were either impossible or not cost-effective without a microcomputer. For instance, a manually maintained file of want-list materials—suffering from "the usual problems of inconsistencies of entry, mis-filing, etc."—was input into an automated system. Slips can be generated automatically, and updating and searching are simple. |
| Significant Problems: | A suggestion is to find others in an institution who are knowledgeable about computers and seek their expertise, or even begin an informal users group to discuss problems. Hard disk storage is needed for sorting large files. |
| Reference: | Harvell, Tony. "Micros in Government Documents Departments," *Small Computers in Libraries*, Dec. 1986, p.29. |
| Project Date(s): | October 1987–Present |
| Cost: | Library operating budget |
| Self-Rating: | 8 |

Name: **Government Documents Processing System**

Library: Fenwick Library, George Mason University

Contact Person: Clyde W. Grotophorst

Address/Phone: Library Systems Office, Fenwick Library, 4400 University Dr., Fairfax, VA 22030; (703) 323-2317

Profile: A university serving approximately 14,500 students and a faculty of 767. The library holdings contain over 236,000 volumes.

Hardware: IBM PC, 256K

Software: *GOVDOC* (written by university staff using *dBase III* (Ashton-Tate) and compiled with *Clipper* (Nantucket). *GOVDOC* may soon be available commercially.

Description: Staff originally used the *Condor 3* (Condor Computer) database management system, but changed to *dBase* for more flexibility. The program was then compiled using *Clipper*, which speeds up execution and makes distribution possible to other libraries that don't own *dBase*. The system was originally created to maintain an online catalog of government documents. Later, the capability for printing reports (listings) of government document holdings was added. Some specific features include: the ability to transfer data between two records, viewing or printing all records found during a search, saving search results to a disk file, maintaining a separate database for deleted records, and making a report on records that have been flagged for deletion. The system will also accurately record SuDoc numbers. The system indexes by SuDoc number, title, and subject fields, making retrieval time less than two seconds in a database of more than 40,000 records.

Significant Problems: None reported

Reference: None available

Project Dates(s): 1985–86

Self-Rating: Not given

Name: **Government Documents Keyword Indexing**

Library: University of Miami Library

Contact Person: Tony Harvell

Address/Phone: University of Miami Library, Box 248214, Coral Gables, FL 33124; (305) 284-3155

Profile: University Library, Government Documents Department

Hardware: IBM PC (OCLC M300), with HardCard

Software: *KWICIE* (library's own program written in BASIC for PC DOS 2.0). This is a copyrighted software, but it is being offered free to interested libraries.

Description:    The primary purpose of this project was to provide "keyword-in-context" indexes of the library's Intergovernmental Organization (IGO) collections, a large, uncataloged document collection. Once the files were computerized, the library could generate a hard copy of the keyword index and a "stoplist." Since the file was so large, the library found it necessary to split it into two parts. The database records all have three fields: title (115 characters), holdings information (20 characters), and location (23 characters). The title field is used for keyword indexing and contains subject terms.

Significant Problems:    None reported

Reference:    None available

Project Date(s):    April 1986–Present

Cost:    Library budget

Self-Rating:    9

# Handicapped Access

Handicapped access to libraries and information has been a growing concern for some time. Most libraries have made some efforts in this direction, with the addition of elevators, talking books, and special parking spaces. The one project in this section shows how it is possible to go even further, making the handicapped person a full partner and participant in the world of knowledge and information.

Name: **Special Needs Center**

Library: Phoenix Public Library

Contact Person: Mary Roatch

Address/Phone: 12 East McDowell Rd., Phoenix, AZ 85004; (602) 261-8695

Profile: The Phoenix Public Library houses more than 1,200,000 volumes and serves a population of 823,000 with an annual circulation of 3,830,000.

Hardware: The Special Needs Center makes available a variety of equipment, including microcomputers and other aids: IBM PC XT with *SynPhonix* (Artic Technologies) or *DecTalk* synthetic speech, dot matrix and letter quality printers, *VersaPoint Braille Embosser*, and *Telephone Device for the Deaf* (TDD).

Software: *BEX* (Raised Dot Computing) to provide large print, braille, and synthetic voice for visually impaired people. *WordTalk, FileTalk, ScreenTalk* (all from Computer Aids) facilitate text to speech access for Apple IIe and IBM. Duxbury braille translation program for the VersaBraille II and IBM. *WordPerfect* (Word Perfect Corporation) for IBM macros developed from *ScreenTalk Pro. MicroInterpreter I and II* (Microtech Consulting) for sign language instruction on the Apple IIe. *inLARGE* (Berkeley System) for the Macintosh, which creates windows of large print for low-vision computer users. *MacWrite* (Apple Computers), *MacPaint* (Apple Computers), and *Ready, Set, Go* (Letraset) for the Macintosh.

Description: The Special Needs Center developed out of the realization that it was difficult for many patrons to make use of traditional library services without special technology. The library has established an Electronic Communications Training Program, which helps blind users to operate the library's computers. Staff and several hundred blind volunteers provide instruction. Once mastered, the students can use their newly acquired computer skills independently, without the presence of a librarian. The lab interfaces new, modern equipment such as the Braille-Editor (a blind person can hear where the cursor is on the monitor and edit text) and the Kurzweil Reading Machine (which allows scanned letters to be read synthetically). Some high school students use the center to do their class reports on the VersaBraille. In addition, users are experimenting with new ways to enhance the machines and operations at the center. For instance, one is experimenting on ways to make bus schedules available in different formats, for example, audible, hard-copy braille, and large type. An editor of a local newspaper for the blind uses the center to produce the publication in braille. The center is used in a wide variety of other ways as well. It is an active and exciting place for people with visual disabilities to receive traditional library services.

Significant Problems: None reported

Reference: Roatch, Mary A. "Electronic Access to Print Information for Blind and Visually Impaired Persons in the Public Library," *Public Computing*, Sept.–Oct. 1986, p.3.

Project Date(s): November 1983–Present

Cost: Federal funding of $150,525; private gifts of $6,185; annual book budget of $12,000; salaries of $131,351. Supplies and maintenance are part of regular operating budget of library.

Self-Rating: 9

# Indexing

*Indexing* refers to keeping track of pamphlet files, local newspapers, or vertical-file materials. The local newspaper index, long the province of the local history of genealogy buff, is ideal for the computer. Indexing programs allow for quick access to data, the printing of name and subject indexes, and even Boolean logic searches. A few of the problems encountered with some projects include lack of sufficient RAM memory if the program is a RAM resident data program and enough volunteers to input the data.

The vertical file or pamphlet file, as cited below, is really more of an acquisitions file than an index to current literature. Tracking what comes in allows the library to make better choices during the next round of requests.

Name: **Local History (Newspaper Index)**
Library: Elmhurst Public Library
Contact Persons: Raita Vilnins and Mary Beth Harnden
Address/Phone: 211 Prospect, Elmhurst, IL 60126; (312) 279-8696
Profile: Serves a population of 44,000; 141,000 volumes and an annual circulation of over 400,000.
Hardware: IBM PC XT, 512K, 20-megabyte hard disk.
Software: The software for such a project should be menu-driven and easy to use. *Finder* (Aaron Smith), the software finally selected, was chosen because it allowed "for the development of an indexing system that was simple and which would also allow for the utilization of the computer to an optimum level, so that most of the work could be done by a clerk." Because of the potential size of the database, a large-enough capacity was needed. *Finder's* only real limit is the size of the hard disk. In addition, *Finder* did free-text or natural language searching, Boolean logic, and truncation. One problem with the software was its print ability. In order to print the index regularly, it was necessary to purchase a program called *Vacalist* for $130. The vendor provided two free hours of consulting time.

Description:   Computerization of newspaper indexing was necessary in order to make it more efficient, provide Boolean logic, and eliminate 3-by-5-inch card files. When the project officially ended (though indexing continues), 113 issues of the *Elmhurst Press* had been indexed using the computer.

Each article requires one screen of data entry, making a grand total (for 113 issues) of 2,469 screens. Between 28 and 32 articles per issue were indexed, with between 4 and 12 descriptors per article, in addition to headline, event date(s), and issue date. A preliminary test showed the computerized retrieval rate to be 18 percent better than the manual counterpart.

Goals established for the project: (1) to determine whether it is possible to undertake a computerized indexing project without expertise in computers; (2) to identify appropriate software and select a program for testing; (3) to determine whether an increase in the number of access points substantially increases the usefulness of the index; (4) to determine how successfully a clerk can be trained to do data entry and assign subject headings from a list; (5) to determine whether computerizing the index increased the demand for it; (6) to use a microcomputer to index local news, both current and retrospectively for one year, thereby creating a basis for comparison with the manual index the library already had in use; (7) to document and disseminate project findings, including recommendations about adopting or modifying commercial software, developing a new program, maintaining a vocabulary control, and developing subject heading authority.

Work is now accomplished 90 percent by clerical staff. Each article to be indexed in each issue is numbered, and descriptors are taken from them. A librarian then assigns broad subject headings. The completed issue is edited by the librarian who then assigns new or additional subject headings. Librarian involvement is kept to a minimum. As of this writing, it had not yet been determined whether or not the computerization had increased demand for it. Total FTE hours reported were 895.32, 46 percent of which was indexing. Inputting and other computer functions required 27 percent. Training required: 10 percent.

Significant Problems:   Considerable computer expertise is required for this type of project. If it is not available, the library should be prepared to hire consultants or programmers. Poor documentation for the software and for DOS also contributed problems. Enough time should be allowed for extensive planning.

Reference: Vilnins, Raita. "Local Newspaper Indexing Project," *Illinois Libraries*, Jan. 1987, p.64.

Project Date(s): September 1985; June 1986 grant

Cost: LSCA grant of $9,325; local funding of $3,336.30. Funds included $4,439.45 for hardware and $1,925 for software.

Self-Rating: 8

Name: **Pamphlet Database**

Library: Shelby State Community College

Contact Person: Joe Lindenfeld

Address/Phone: Box 40568, Memphis, TN 38174; (901) 528-6743

Profile: The college has an enrollment of approximately 3,300 and holdings of more than 60,000 titles. Four professional staff, six clerical, and four student assistants.

Hardware: Apple IIe, two disk drives.

Software: *AppleWorks* (Apple Computers)

Description: This simple project proved to be very useful, providing additional access points for vertical-file materials. The database works thusly: Dewey decimal numbers are assigned to all new pamphlets, which are then placed in one of 267 on-shelf pamphlet boxes. To improve access, one to five subjects are assigned to each box title. (Example: 327 International Relations—Middle East; SADAT-BEGIN CONFERENCE; ISRAEL; JEWISH-ARAB RELATIONS; ARAB COUNTRIES; LEBANON). Once all entries have been made—entry may be in random order—*AppleWorks* allows quick and easy rearrangement of subject headings by Dewey number, pamphlet box title, or any subject field. In the article cited below, detailed instructions are given for creating a combined index for all five subject fields. Depending upon how much RAM is available, this system for keeping track of pamphlet titles and subjects could be expanded to contain many more entries.

Significant Problems: None reported

Reference: Lindenfeld, Joe. "Indexing a Pamphlet Database Using *AppleWorks*," *Apple Library Users Group Newsletter*, Oct. 1987, p.62.

Project Date(s): September 1986–March 1987

Cost: No additional funding required

Self-Rating: 7

Name: **Vertical File**

Library: College of Saint Scholastica Library

Contact Person:  Rachel Applegate

Address/Phone:  1200 Kenwood Ave., Duluth, MN 55811; (218) 723-6178

Profile:  The College of St. Scholastica teaches special medical programs in nursing, geriatrics, and dietetics to approximately 1,100 students. The library maintains a collection of 100,000 volumes and employs four full professional and three paraprofessional librarians.

Hardware:  IBM-compatible PC (Zenith), two disk drives.

Software:  *WordStar* (MicroPro), already owned.

Description:  The vertical file is often a collection of folders that are difficult to organize. Knowing what kind of new materials to order or what to weed can be just as problematic. This project used a word-processing package to track vertical-file material orders to determine the response success rate. Using *WordStar*, a file is created that contains suppliers of free materials, entered by first keyword (e.g., "Minnesota Department of Forestry" is found under "Forestry"). A request date is also appended to each record to make it possible to determine how long it takes suppliers to reply, if at all. As the requested materials are received by the library, a count is made of usable items from each supplier. A subject file printout is used to assign subjects to the newly arrived materials. The number of usable items from each supplier is added to the supplier file, along with date received. One other file (BROWSER.PAM) maintains a list of pamphlet material received arranged by subject heading, along with short descriptions of each. Using this list, staff is able to pinpoint weaknesses and improve weeding of the collection. It was reported that this system cuts normal vertical file-processing time in half and increases timeliness.

Significant Problems:  None reported. One improvement suggested, however, included adding a file to track "standing-order" sources of materials.

Reference:  Applegate, Rachel. "*WordStar* and the Vertical File," *Small Computers in Libraries*, July 1987, p.41.

Project Date(s):  December 1986–January 1987 (design stage).

Cost:  Since hardware and software were already owned, there were only mailing costs.

Self-Rating:  10

# Interlibrary Loan

Interlibrary loan (ILL) presents many problems for libraries, at least a few of which can be alleviated with the aid of computerization. Any telecommunications system that allows for the exchange of ILL data will help.

Name: **ILL Data Collection**

Library: Colorado State University Libraries

Contact Person: Robert W. Burns

Address/Phone: William E. Morgan Library, CO 80532

Profile: Serving an enrollment of nearly 20,000, the library has holdings of 1,400,000 books and periodical subscriptions.

Hardware: NCR PC 6 Model 1015 (MS-DOS), 640K RAM, one floppy drive, 10-megabyte hard drive (streamer tape backup, Okidata 193 full carriage printer).

Software: *Symphony 1.1* (Lotus Development)

Description: This project used the standard spreadsheet *Symphony 1.1* to facilitate the preparation of a monthly interlibrary loan statistical report. The monthly report contains four tables: "Library Codes," "Items Borrowed," "Items Loaned," and "Master Statistical Summary." Special care was taken to facilitate data entry so that, once complete, the spreadsheet would perform a variety of statistical, arithmetical and other functions, including alphabetization of the file. Some shorthand methods saved time; a three-letter code was entered and translated by the program into the full library name, total year-to-date summaries, "run comparisons, and transfer of monthly data to the annual statistical summary report."

Significant Problems: None given

Reference: *Library Software Review*, Dec. 1987, p.372.

Project Date(s): Not given

Cost: Not given

Self-Rating: Not given

Name: **ILL Journal Request File**
Library: Cullom–Davis Library, Bradley University
Contact Persons: Susan Eichelberger/Marina Savoie
Address/Phone: 1501 W. Bradley Ave., Peoria, IL 61625
Profile: The library serves a student body of 5,500 and a faculty of more than 270. Holdings include 350,000 book volumes and 2,300 periodical subscriptions. The nearly 100 staff members include 9 professionals and 64 student assistants.
Hardware: IBM PC with hard disk drive
Software: *dBase III* (Ashton-Tate)
Description: Project essentially transferred a paper file of interlibrary loan journal requests to a microcomputer database system, *dBase III*. The six-year-old paper file of request forms filled out by patrons was becoming difficult to manage and it was believed that it could be handled more efficiently on a microcomputer. The *dBase III* program also possessed the capacity to handle the estimated 6,500 titles in the paper file, though the IBM PC did not (it had to be upgraded with a hard disk drive). Using the manual method, which was considered to be an efficient system, a patron request was entered on the form and then processed, including available locations, ISBN number, OCLC record number, etc. This record is maintained permanently, and when a second request is made for the same title, there is no need to search for all of the information. This also provides the library with a permanent record of requests to comply with the copyright guidelines. Sixteen fields in all are used in the *dBase* database.
Significant Problems: Problems that occurred included limitations on *dBase's* ability to perform string searches, as well as its sensitivity to upper- and lowercase, which, for retrieval purposes, makes it necessary to input all journal titles in uppercase. (Newer versions of the program or other database systems may solve these problems.)
Reference: *Library Software Review*, Aug. 1987, p.178.
Project Date(s): 1986–87 startup
Cost: Computer already owned, but upgraded with a hard disk drive for this project.
Self-Rating: Not given

Name: **ILL Use of an Electronic Bulletin Board System**
Library: Wisconsin Interlibrary Services
Contact Person: Cathy Moore

Address/Phone: Room 464, 728 State St., Madison, WI 53706; (608) 262-0047

Profile: Provides interlibrary loan, document delivery, resource sharing, and other services for 56 member academic libraries, 7 special, 19 public, and the Wisconsin Division for Library Services.

Hardware: IBM PC with 10-megabyte hard disk, AST 6-Pack Plus board (memory board for 640K total), Epson FX 80+ printer, and Hayes Smartmodem 1200.

Software: RBBS (user supported, available through Capital PC Users Group for about $6); *PC Talk* (PC-SIG); *DoubleDOS* (SoftLogic Solutions, time sharing program). *PrintQ* (Software Directions), a print spooler. Various programs were customized and various new routines were written to improve the system.

Description: Wisconsin Interlibrary Services is a hub for the transmission of interlibrary loan services between libraries. This project is perhaps the most spectacular use of a microcomputer electronic bulletin board system for interlibrary loan. It was conceived because "TWX machines were costly and paper-based ILL communications were too slow and lacked the flexibility of electronic request." Project director Cathy Moore has not only been a superb manager but a fine programmer as well. Furthermore, she has taken the time to document her work in a number of articles and through conference talks. The system now handles some 90,000 ILL requests and saves approximately 94 percent of the transmission costs of the TWX system it replaces. This has led to the use of many such boards in Wisconsin.

Significant Problems: Do not assume that RBBS is the right program for the job. Some trial-and-error and research may lead to a different choice. Avoid systems that require programming.

Reference: Moore, Cathy. "Do-It-Yourself Automation: Interloan Bulletin Boards," *Library Journal*, Nov. 1, 1987, p.66.

Project Date(s): May 1985–Present

Cost: Not given

Self-Rating: 8

# Local Area Networks

A local area network (LAN) allows two or more microcomputers to join forces by using the same memory, peripherals, and hard-disk drives. Users may also exchange documents and electronic mail directly; for example, a user in the science library may query someone in the biology department about an interlibrary loan, the details of a reference question, a book purchase, etc. as long as the two are linked on the LAN. Such "correspondence" may be received instantly, or it may be held by the computer until the person to whom it is sent returns from a coffee break, etc. The computers are cabled together and require special LAN software and hardware in order to function properly. It may take the assistance of a consultant to decide upon the type of system and how to go about getting it installed, since the number of options available is great. Installation is becoming less difficult with the advent of new systems for the Apple- and IBM-compatible computers. (Anyone contemplating a LAN should look into these first, since they make self-installation possible for librarians with the time and inclination.) A major problem with LANs has always been their prohibitive cost, but a big drop in prices has made them fall within the range of smaller libraries. As a result, a growing number of libraries are installing such systems. Very small libraries have a difficult time justifying such a communication system, since they work best in those libraries that are spread out into distinct departments set apart geographically, either on different floors or in different buildings.

| | |
|---:|:---|
| Name: | **LAN in a Hospital Library** |
| Library: | Allegheny General Hospital |
| Contact Person: | Susan B. Hoehl |
| Address/Phone: | 320 East North Ave., Pittsburgh, PA 15212; (412) 359-3040 |
| Profile: | A health sciences library with 3,700 book titles and 410 periodical subscriptions. Three professional staff and five nonprofessional. |
| Hardware: | IBM PCs with 76-megabyte hard disk. |
| Software: | *Netware* (Novell), *WordStar* (MicroPro) for word process- |

ing, *dBase II* (Ashton-Tate) for database management, *Datalog: Acquisitions*, *Catalog*, *Serials* for library functions.

Description: This project was inspired by the desire to build a multi-user, multi-task system to automate departmental and user activities in the library for greater efficiency, enhance communications with other hospitals, and provide an online catalog that allows users to perform their own database searching. Staff was fully involved in the planning process, and though some had experience with computers, it did not particularly help in this "start from scratch" operation. While LANs are generally very complex operations, their components are basically divided into needs analysis, system alternatives analysis, installation and implementation, and the appointment of a network supervisor. The first step, needs analysis, provided an opportunity for the staff to analyze the types of users that would effect the system, the functions likely to be performed, and the availability of workstations to perform such work. Three alternatives were considered, a LAN being only one. (A multiuser multiprocessing system and a time-sharing system were the other two.) A LAN was chosen on the basis of several factors: data-sharing requirements, the need to link all hospital users (ultimately) to the library system, "the determination that the hospital mainframe had no available storage and processing space," and the need for onsite control of the system. Ideally a system should concentrate on selected applications software first, then hardware, and finally a network; but as a practical matter it must all be done at approximately the same time. Once selections have been made, it is necessary to have a dealer do the actual physical installation and cabling of the system (as part of the purchase price). Many vendors will also help in the loading of the software, the addition of the applications packages, and even user training. A network supervisor, it is stressed, should be responsible for keeping a general watch over the entire system, including training, trouble-shooting, and even creating batch files and user menus. The "costs and benefits" of this system have been the central database of library holdings, increased user access, and the ease of adding to or updating the database.

Significant Problems: One of the major problems noted is the lack of sufficient applications software; much of what can be purchased off-the-shelf simply won't function on a LAN (or function poorly). Single CPU (central processing unit) license agreement software may also be a violation when used on a network. Vendor and dealer support is also generally unreliable.

Reference: Angier, Jennifer, and Hoehl, Susan B. "Local Area Networks (LAN) in the Special Library: Part 1—A Planning Model," *Online*, Nov. 1986, p.19. ("Part 2—Implementation" appeared in the same issue, p.29.)

Project Date(s): 1983–85

Cost: Private foundation money for $45,000

Self-Rating: 8

Name: **Library Circulation and Inventory on a LAN**

Library: Kentucky Talking Book Library

Contact Person: Richard Feindel

Address/Phone: Box 537, Frankfort, KY 40602; (502) 875-7000

Profile: The Talking Book Library is part of the Special Services Branch within the Field Services Division of the Kentucky Department for Libraries and Archives, which is the state library agency in Kentucky. KTBL is also a part of a national network of libraries serving the handicapped.

Hardware: IBM PCs, ATs, and AT clones, 90-megabyte hard disk, UPS, 60-megabyte cartridge backup system, OCR words.

Software: *Advanced Netware* (Novell), 286SFT Level II, MS-DOS 3.21 (Microsoft), *READS* version 2.0., a custom software package for libraries serving the blind and physically handicapped who are using materials from the Library of Congress. It was developed by Mobius Management Systems of New Rochelle, N.Y., for the Library of Congress, National Library Service for the Blind and Physically Handicapped.

Description: This project began as a solution to the backlog in circulation, staff shortages, and the need to move beyond manual records. Extensive consultation with software developers was required throughout the project. Specifically, the project was implemented under the auspices of the Kentucky Talking Book Library (KTBL), which provides public library services to print-handicapped individuals and uses a local area network. This IBM PC–based LAN allows for the use of READS, an integrated inventory and circulation system. The results of this system have been a 40 percent increase in circulation and streamlined internal procedures. READS (Reader Enrollment and Delivery System) contains modules that will register patrons, catalog books and magazines, automate circulation, and inventory tape units.

It also automatically interfaces with the library's national mailing list database.

Significant Problems: A LAN was found to place more stress on hardware elements of the system than stand-alone products or systems, causing more frequent breakdowns. Because of the ability to swap various elements of the system without difficulty, there were no maintenance charges and the staff has been able to do everything themselves. Other problems, such as electrical storms, were also reported.

Reference: None available

Project Date(s): February 4, 1985–Present

Cost: LSCA grant for $36,000

Self-Rating: 10

# Management

Name: **Salary Increases Using a Microcomputer**
Library: Oregon Health Sciences University Libraries
Contact Person: Millard F. Johnson, Jr.
Address/Phone: 3181 S.W. Sam Jackson Park Rd., Box 573, Portland, OR 97207
Profile: Serves nearly 1,600 students and 650 faculty. A staff of twenty-nine maintains a collection of over 160,000 volumes and 2,200 periodical subscriptions, with a special collection in the history of medicine.
Hardware: IBM or compatible
Software: *Visicalc* (VisiCorp), *Framework II* (Ashton-Tate) spreadsheet module.
Description: This project used a microcomputer spreadsheet to attempt to objectively assign salary increases, relating them to inflation, merit, and equity (current value of the employee to the library). While the calculations and variables performed to reach this end are too lengthy to be described here, they do involve assigning variables in experience, difficulty of work, initiative, local cost of living, inflation, equity adjustment, and merit adjustment. Recommended for anyone wishing to set up a spreadsheet model that will allow users to take many variables into account when assigning salaries.
Reference: Johnson, Millard F. ''An Objective Method for Allocating Salary Increases,'' *Library Software Review*, Nov.–Dec. 1987, p.354.
Project Date(s): Spring 1985–Present
Cost: Not given
Self-Rating: Not given

Name: **Maintaining Subscriber Files**
Library: Merriam Center Library

Contact Person: Dennis Jenks

Address/Phone: 1313 E. 60th St., Chicago, IL 60637; (312) 947-2165

Profile: The Charles E. Merriam Library was established more than 50 years ago and serves a group of nonprofit organizations in Chicago's Hyde Park area, including the American Planning Association, American Public Works Association, students and faculty of the University of Chicago, and the general public. The collection contains over 50,000 monographs, 100,000 reports, 800 periodical titles, and 1,000 annual and irregular serials.

Hardware: Macintosh SE, 40-megabyte hard disk drive, Imagewriter II.

Software: *Microsoft File v. 1.05* (Microsoft)

Description: Facilitating billing of subscribers to the center's newsletter was the primary purpose of using *Microsoft File* to create a subscriber database. While a more powerful database management system (according to staff) would improve the system, it was still possible to create a file that automatically generated invoices. A major problem encountered was the difficulty in generating a separate copy for retention at the library. This DBMS works well with files under 1,000 records in length.

Significant Problems: None reported

Reference: None available

Project Date(s): Winter 1986

Cost: Library budget, $3,400

Self-Rating: 5

Name: **Space Planning and Collection Analysis with *Enable***

Library: University Library, University of California at Santa Cruz

Contact Person: Steven Watkins

Address/Phone: Santa Cruz, CA 95604; (408) 459-2886

Profile: 220,000 volumes. Serves 3,500 students and 150 faculty.

Hardware: IBM PC XT, 640K, 20-megabyte hard disk.

Software: *Enable* (The Software Group), an integrated software package, though any spreadsheet that can handle 50 columns by 100 rows will work. Staff was familiar with *Enable*, thus saving on training time.

Description: This project applied a spreadsheet modeling system to the space planning required by the libraries as collections outgrew buildings and shelving. Specifically, *Enable* was purchased "to develop a set of interrelated spreadsheets that model the science collection at UC Santa Cruz." This collection is approximately 190,000 volumes, but only half can be housed in the science library, with the remainder kept across campus in the main library. Since 10,000 volumes are added each year, it is necessary to move an equal number to the main library. The spreadsheet allows this to be done equitably by making percentage calculations of how much of each department's collection is shelved at the main versus the science library. Circulation statistics and user population from each department can also be correlated at the same time. This quantitative analysis of the collections can be used in decision making for collection transfer. In addition the spreadsheet may be used to determine how the remaining space will be appropriated once selected materials have been removed. The process begins by mapping each floor of the building on a spreadsheet, including the LC class number size of each section, amount of material to be moved, and the volumes to be added annually. By extrapolating the likely size of each collection with this data, the library may then determine just how much shelf space will be needed for each LC section. Another project utilizes this data to make a twenty-year space-requirement projection, which will play a role in the construction planning now in progress for a new science library.

Significant Problems: None reported

Reference: See *Small Computers in Libraries Proceedings* (Meckler, 1987) for executive summary.

Project Date(s): 1985–87

Cost: Hardware already in place. Software purchased with grant from Librarian's Association of the University of California: $340.

Self-Rating: 8

Name: **Stack Management**

Library: Farrell Library, Kansas State University

Contact Person: Rachel S. Moreland

Address/Phone: Manhattan, Kansas 66506; (913) 539-8713

Profile: This university has an enrollment of over 18,000 and a faculty of 2,215. Total book collection exceeds 900,000 volumes, with 8,000 periodical subscriptions.

Hardware: Zenith, two disk drives.

Software: *SuperCalc3* (Sorcim), already owned.

Description: This exciting project's main goal was to make predictions about the growth of stack space in order to properly redistribute or reshelve the collection so that no additional changes would be necessary for ten years. These projections could also be used for collection development. After a literature search, which turned up only one citation about computers and stack management, the library set about creating its own program on a spreadsheet. Since shelf space is filled with new acquisitions at an uneven rate, the most important information that was required in order to accomplish the project was the number of monographs received in each Library of Congress category during the preceding five years (this was assumed to be a long enough period to chart any trend). Data were obtained from the library's OCLC archive tapes, as was information on the growth of serials through actual bindery reports and the library's automated serials list. The actual shelving available and the total occupied space were measured. In order to calculate the "monograph average size" (width), 385 books in each LC category were measured. The spreadsheet must first calculate the entire amount of free space in the collection before percentage allocations can be made for individual categories. A second spreadsheet into which acquisitions data are entered determines "new occupied space" and "remaining free space."

| | |
|---|---|
| Significant Problems: | None reported |
| Reference: | *Small Computers in Libraries*, June 1987, p.38. |
| Project Date(s): | 1986–87 |
| Cost: | No additional funds required |
| Self-Rating: | 6 |

| | |
|---|---|
| Name: | **Local History Collection Survey** |
| Library: | Maywood Public Library/Suburban Library System |
| Contact Person: | Patrick R. Dewey |
| Address/Phone: | 121 S. Fifth Ave., Maywood, IL 60153; (312) 343-1847 |
| Profile: | Maywood Public Library serves a community of approximately 28,000 residents, approximately 70 percent black, the remainder split between Hispanic and white. It has one branch library (storefront) and one main library. The Suburban Library System is a multitype system just west of Chicago, encompassing approximately 180 libraries. |
| Hardware: | Apple IIe, with RAMworks III (memory expansion board with 256K), Zenith 148, 728K RAM, Canon printer. |
| Software: | *AppleWorks* (Apple Computers) word-processing module and *WordPerfect* (WordPerfect). |
| Description: | No listing of local history resources in the Suburban Library System existed, and it was decided to survey the participating libraries and print out the results for distribution and mount them electronically on Lincolnet, the system's BBS. Once initial work collecting data was com- |

pleted, it had to be input into an electronic system, using *AppleWorks*. Data were mounted on Lincolnet as a simple ASCII text file and then downloaded to a staff member's home for use as a MS-DOS file for work on *WordPerfect*. Use of this word-processing system made global changes and corrections much faster and permitted the creation of an index of libraries and resources.

Significant Problems:  RAMworks expansion board and incompatibility with RGB color monitor.

Reference:  None available

Project Date(s):  1987–88

Cost:  None required

Self-Rating:  8

# Online Catalogs and Catalog Cards

The projects in this section range from simple—automating the production of catalog cards with the correct punctuation—to more complex, such as compiling CD-ROM union catalogs of statewide resources. Catalogs produced on a microcomputer need not be online, though having an online catalog can produce efficient search capabilities and makes the product easy to update. Offline catalogs, those that are produced as a printout once the data entry has been completed and indexed, are useful as giveaways to patrons or as desk catalogs for staff or public. Some catalogs help school libraries maintain control over audiovisual collections. In addition, small public libraries keep running inventories of their videotape collections.

| | |
|---|---|
| Name: | **Catalog Cards** |
| Library: | Maywood Public Library |
| Contact Person: | Kristin Flanders |
| Address/Phone: | 121 S. Fifth Ave., Maywood, IL 60153; (312) 343-1847 |
| Profile: | Maywood Public Library serves a community of approximately 28,000 residents, approximately 70 percent black, the remainder split between Hispanic and white. It has one branch library (storefront) and one main library. |
| Hardware: | Apple IIe, two disk drives, Imagewriter printer (later added Printex printer). |
| Software: | *Librarian's Helper* (Scarecrow) |
| Description: | The Maywood Public Library had long used a memory typewriter to generate catalog cards for books that did not come preprocessed from the vendor. Several years ago, however, the person who had memorized the AACR2 punctuation and rules left the library. Also, the memory typewriter ceased functioning. Since an Apple was now available, it was decided to consider the value of several catalog card programs. Many were tried, but few had the flexibility of *Librarian's Helper*. One of the major advan- |

tages to this system is its ability to "kill" fields not used, making data entry easier.

Significant Problems:  A major problem was the actual printing of the cards, since the Imagewriter was not equipped to deal with card stock. Thinner card stock was tried, but this created problems of its own (including the paper peeling apart as it passed through the printer). The solution was a "bottom-feed" printer, i.e., one that accepts paper from underneath so that card stock does not have to bend and curl around the platen. Such bending and curling often causes dragging.

Reference:  None available

Project Date(s):  1987–Present

Cost:  No additional funds needed. Software from regular library AV budget.

Name:  **Computerized Media Catalog**

Library:  Educational Studies, University of Missouri–St. Louis

Contact Person:  Dennis K. Smeltzer

Address/Phone:  262 Marillac, 8001 Natural Bridge Rd., St. Louis, MO 63121; (314) 553-5941

Profile:  The University of Missouri at St. Louis has 12,000 students and a faculty of 400. Major resources are the Thomas Jefferson Library, with 250,000 book titles, and the Education Library, with approximately 25,000 book titles.

Hardware:  IBM PC, 640K, Epson LQ1500 printer, Tallgrass 35-megabyte hard disk. (Minimum hardware required: Apple IIe, 128K, 80-column card, two disk drives, dot matrix printer.)

Software:  *Smart Database* (Innovative Software) was used since it was already owned.

Description:  The project was developed while Dennis K. Smeltzer was director of audiovisual services for the St. Louis Public Schools, which had a collection of more than 17,000 AV titles. Every two or three years a catalog of the collection was produced commercially. That still left the rather formidable problem of dealing with some $100,000 in new materials purchases each year, materials that were not accessible to teachers until the next catalog was published. The goal was to produce frequent and inexpensive catalog supplements. As the project proceeded, it became clear that subject- and grade-specific catalogs and catalogs for individual teachers could also be published with relative ease, allowing the center to meet the needs of its clientele to a greater degree. Most IBM database programs will do the job, as will the Apple program *AppleWorks*. The more powerful the system, however, the more that can be done. The data fields used in the AV collection file are divided into "Medium Related Fields" (catalog/call number, title, sort title, producer, production/copyright date, media format, running time, audience level, various subject areas and description lines) and "Administrative Related Fields" (item cost, number of copies, total value of title, vendor, date of acquisition, condition, date of removal). Planning must be done carefully in order to ensure that the fields are those that best serve the library. Once data have been input, various reports can be generated, including the title report with subject listings. Many types of lists can be produced simply with most database systems. The type of subject listings may vary considerably, however. For example, using *PFS* (a database system), a subject listing can be printed out by sorting by subject field and then by title, but each title may only be listed once, even though it may have several subjects. More powerful systems, such as *dBase III+*, will allow for multiple subject listings and even an exchange of data or interaction between different files (relational database systems that compare or handle two files at once). The final product is camera-ready copy for the local print shop, which produces the printed catalog.

Significant Problems: Buy the right database management system (DBMS) for your needs, input new data in batches to save time, use upper- and lowercase letters if possible (it will make the catalog look better and easier to read), use subject headings consistently, enter series of media titles together by using the same initial words (e.g., "Dr. Doolittle—Counting, Part I"; "Dr. Doolittle—Counting, Part II"), have two different people proofread everything, include instructions on the use of the catalog for the client, make full use of the DBMS by printing out special catalogs for seasonal materials (or even a videotape catalog).

Reference: *Small Computers in Libraries*, Sept. 1987, p.18.

Project Date(s): Dec. 1985–Sept. 1986

Cost: Existing hardware and software were used requiring no additional expense. Some 8,000 sixty-page catalogs were printed locally for $500. The cost for 6,000 copies of a commercial catalog is about $15,000.

Self-rating: Not given

Name: **Online Catalog for Media Center**
Library: Sage Learning Center, Bronx Community College

Contact Person: Annette Peretz

Address/Phone: W. 181st St. and University Ave., Bronx, NY 10453; (212) 220-6190

Profile: Sage Learning Center is a model educational program for 7,000 nontraditional students with varied learning requirements involving basic skills deficiencies, ESL difficulties, etc. The students are, however, highly motivated by a desire to acquire a college education.

Hardware: One Zenith AT/compatible, 40-megabyte hard drive (for student searching); two Zenith XTs with 20-megabyte hard drive for inputting, editing, and librarian use for searching and reports; two Epson printers (one LQ 800, one FX 286E), used for mini-catalogs, subject printouts.

Software: *COMPULOG* (Embar Information Consultants), originally selected because of price, flexibility, and ease of customization. The program evolved into *COMPULOG MEDIA*.

Description: Nonprint materials have a variety of access problems. For instance, materials such as videotapes, filmstrips, slide sets, audiocassettes, and even microcomputer software "do not respond well to conventional cataloging," they cannot be browsed, and they have no indexes or tables of contents. Furthermore, conventional subject headings are inadequate for searching them. The final product was a locally produced online catalog. Work entailed finding a suitable database system, creating the right type of data record for users, and re-cataloging the 10,000 plus items in the collection. The original consultant, though enthusiastic, determined that the library could not afford such a catalog and suggested using the standard *COMPULOG* product. The library rejected this suggestion and asked the Embar associates to customize *COMPULOG* for print and nonprint materials. A two-year LSCA Title III grant was obtained. The result was an easy-to-use, menu-driven program that only requires filling in a template workform. (Any staff person can perform this function with little training.) Once an entry had been made, however, it later had to be edited and proofread. Assigning and refining subject headings was the most difficult task, and it was performed by librarians who had to be trained to re-catalog with more detailed contents and natural language subject headings. It is even possible to make global changes in subject headings. Future plans include cross-references. At present, staff use a printout of keywords and cross-references taken from the subject authority list. Staff report that this "project is ideal for school media centers, instructional materials centers,

LRCs, special library collections, films, music, slides— anything without a table of contents and index.''

Significant Problems: In order to save time, it is suggested that the collection be thoroughly weeded or re-catalog the most important items first. Otherwise, the presence of many items no longer of value will slow the entry process.

Reference: None available

Project Date(s): 1986–Present

Cost: U.S. Department of Education under LSCA Title III.

Name: **MARC Record Staff Development Program**

Library: University of Missouri–Columbia School of Library and Informational Science

Contact Person: Frederick J. Raithel

Address/Phone: 104 Stewart Hall, School of Library and Informational Science, University of Missouri–Columbia, Columbia, MO 65211; (314) 882-9543

Profile: ALA-accredited graduate library school

Hardware: M300 (IBM PC)

Software: BASIC programming language

Description: This useful program was written as a visual aid for teaching librarians and library students about MARC record formats. It is not interactive; the student does not use the program for a hands-on exercise. The instructor will prompt the program during a lecture to detail the next section on the monitor or screen being viewed by the class. The program itself ''retrieves and displays cataloging records that are formatted according to the national MARC standard as used in the *BiblioFile* (The Library Corporation) laser disc cataloging system.'' The user must first create a data file by saving approximately ten *BiblioFile* records and then use the upgrade utility to create MARC records. The data are stored in a file called COM.CP. The program then pulls apart the MARC records into their major components: (1) the leader, (2) the record directories, and (3) the bibliographic cataloging data. It is a short program, written in BASICA (IBM format). It is copyrighted, but is offered by the author, Frederick J. Raithel, as ''freeware'' or ''shareware,'' so long as there is no profit involved in its transfer. As written, the program demonstrates the concept of a MARC-formatted record and is intended for staff instructional development. It may be modified further for other applications. The entire program is reproduced in the April 1987 issue of *Small Computers in Libraries* (p.34–35).

Significant Problems: None reported

Reference: Raithel, Frederick J. "READMARC: A Simple BASIC Program to Read MARC Bibliographic Records," *Small Computers in Libraries*, Apr. 1987, p.33.

Project Date(s): 1986–87

Cost: None required

Self-Rating: 10

Name: **Statewide CD-ROM Union Catalog**

Library: Pennsylvania State Library

Contact Person: Richard E. Cassel

Address/Phone: 333 Market St., Harrisburg, PA 17108; (717) 787-6704

Profile: System serves 5,000 academic, public, school, and special libraries with over 100 million volumes.

Hardware: Brodart LePac System; Tandy 1000SX microcomputer and Hitachi 2500S CD-ROM drives.

Software: ACCESS PENNSYLVANIA CD-ROM database (CD-ROM disk and floppy disk search software).

Description: The purpose of this project was to use the power of the CD-ROM to generate a union catalog, which would allow school librarians access to the statewide resource-sharing system. To reach this goal, consultants were called in and a number of systems and technologies were examined to determine which would best meet these needs. The compact disc was selected as the technology that came closest to this goal. The two major objectives were: provide all library users with information about resources throughout Pennsylvania; facilitate library management functions (cataloging, inventory control, circulation, etc.), freeing up librarians to work directly with patrons. As a result, patrons can now search through full MARC records for information contained in nearly 200 libraries and then receive the books, journals, or other materials through interlibrary loan. The impact of this technology and access to information has, according to those involved, varied according to the type and size of library. School libraries have reported as much as a 300 to 500 percent increase in circulation because of the ease with which patrons can now browse vast holdings of resources (and also because of the more sophisticated search capabilities of CD-ROM). More than one million unique titles are now contained in this database.

Significant Problems: None reported

Reference: Epler, Doris M., and Cassel, Richard E. "ACCESS PENN-

SYLVANIA: A CD-ROM Database Project,'' *Library Hi Tech*, No.19, p.81.

Project Date(s): 1985–Present

Cost: First-year costs were $400,000 in federally funded money.

Self-Rating: Not given

Name: **Specialized Information Center**

Library: San Jose Public Library (Silicon Valley Information Center)

Contact Person: Sharon D. Cline

Address/Phone: 180 W. San Carlos St., San Jose, CA 95113 (Cline is a sales representative for EBSCO Subscription Services.)

Profile: The San Jose Public Library has an annual circulation of over 2.75 million and serves more than 670,000 persons. It has a staff of 200 and over 1.2 million volumes.

Hardware: Four IBM XTs, one IBM AT.

Software: *dBase III* (Ashton-Tate), *VolksWriter 3* (Lifetree Software).

Description: The center was conceived as a resource for assisting patrons of the San Jose Public Library who needed data ''related to the people, companies, and products of the high-tech industry in the area.'' ''Digging'' for this information was done in no standard way, and in no single location, thus making searching generally difficult. After considerable investigation, it was decided that the center was the answer to the problem, and a planning grant was obtained from the California State Library. Two LSCA grants over the next two years, along with contributions from the city and corporations, made the center possible. In designing the center, needs focused on an online public access catalog (OPAC) for users and word processing and database management for internal functions on both micro- and minicomputers. The OPAC contains records of a variety of materials, including books, reports, photos, videotapes, films, newsletters, memos, and clippings. All materials are entered into the OPAC. Most of the materials in the center are nonbook materials.

Significant Problems: None reported

Reference: Cline, Sharon D. ''Starting from Scratch in a Specialized Information Center.'' *Library Software Review*, Nov.–Dec. 1987, p.359.

Project Date(s): The center began operation on September 4, 1986.

Cost: Grants totaling nearly $1 million

Self-Rating: Not given

Name: **Media Catalog**

Library: Fenwick Library, George Mason University

Contact Person: Clyde W. Grotophorst

Address/Phone: Library Systems Office, Fenwick Library, 4400 University Dr., Fairfax, VA 22030; (703) 323-2317

Profile: George Mason University has approximately 14,500 students and a faculty of 767. The library holdings number over 236,000 book volumes.

Hardware: IBM PC AT, 640K, 20-megabyte hard drive.

Software: *Personal Librarian* (KNM Associates; formerly SIRE). It supports full text searching, user-defined fields, and variable-length records.

Description: The library's integrated system proved to be inadequate for music information searching; specifically, it would not support a data search in "Contents" notes (MARC tag 505) nor support keyword searching. To overcome this problem, a separate AV card catalog had been developed. Printed lists of music appearing on various recordings were also created. It was eventually decided to take the data from the online catalog and "dump" it into a microcomputer to support sophisticated retrieval methods. This "media catalog," which has approximately 7,000 records, is now updated quarterly. Since the library used the *ALIS II* (Data Phase) system, a program was written in MIIS (the interpreted language of *ALIS*), which would copy information from the *ALIS II* bibliographic database into a Data General MV8000. *Smartcom II* (Hayes), a telecommunications package, was used to transfer the data at 1200 baud to an IBM PC AT. The procedures (and program) were further refined to transfer only certain MARC tags into the new database: Call Number—one of either 099, 090, 050; Author—100, 110; Title—240, 245; Imprint—300; Contents Notes—505; Subject(s)—650; and Added Entries—700, 710. Even after managing to transfer the appropriate information into an MS-DOS format, there remained the problem of transferring the information into a database management system for proper use. Some of the factors considered in the search process were storage, format conversion, and searching. *Personal Librarian* was chosen for several reasons, including the fact that it supports full-text searching and allows user-defined fields as well as variable-length records. The finished product, an online catalog of music information, makes data retrieval much more efficient than it was with the card system it replaces.

| | |
|---|---|
| Significant Problems: | None reported. Readers should note, however, that programming by staff was required for this project. It was also reported in the returned survey that "while our application involved writing MIIS programs to dump data from our integrated system, other libraries might consider using OCLC 'saved-screens,' *BiblioFile* (The Library Corporation), or some other source of bibliographic information for the database. Saved in ASCII form, the file could then be formatted for *Personal Librarian* either by simple BASIC programs or a word processor." |
| Reference: | Grotophorst, Clyde W. "MIIS to MS-DOS: Microcomputer Options for Online Catalog Support," *Library Software Review*, June 1986, p.144. |
| Project Date(s): | 1986–Present |
| Cost: | Library automation budget: $1,700 to $2,500 for hardware; $600 for software. |
| Self-Rating: | 10 |

| | |
|---|---|
| Name: | **AV Catalog Produced from Database** |
| Library: | Winston–Dillard Public School District #116 |
| Contact Person: | Cheryl Page |
| Address/Phone: | Box 288, Dillard, OR 97432; (503) 679-3121 ext. 20 |
| Profile: | This small, rural school district consists of three elementary schools, one middle school, and one high school. |
| Hardware: | Apple IIe, two disk drives, Imagewriter II (RAMworks II or hard drive necessary). |
| Software: | *AppleWorks* (Apple Computers). Selected because of staff experience with the program and compatibility with entire district. |
| Description: | This microcomputer-produced paper AV catalog uses the database component of *AppleWorks* to provide quick access to the software in the Winston–Dillard public schools for teachers and interlibrary loan of materials without formal cataloging. More than 500 programs were entered into the database. Each entry contains call number, name, subject, grade level, media description (disk, guides, etc.), computer type, and a brief annotation. The catalog is arranged in several ways, including by size of school. School locations are also accessible through title and subject indexes. Other catalogs have been produced in a similar manner, one for professional library titles, and one for books in the instructional media center. |
| Significant Problems: | If the collection is very large a RAM card of some type must be used to provide additional memory. |

Reference:  None available
Project Date(s):  September 1986
Cost:  Equipment originally purchased for other functions. Printing costs, $300.
Self-Rating:  10

# Online Search Management

Name: **Working with Downloaded Medline Search Results**

Library: Ohio State University Health Sciences Library

Contact Person: Peter M. LePoer

Address/Phone: Columbus, Ohio 43210

Profile: University library

Hardware: IBM PC

Software: *QModem* (PC-SIG), shareware (copyrighted software that may be freely distributed for preview purposes) telecommunications package; *STAR* (Cuadra Associates), text-oriented database management system.

Description: University staff use a microcomputer for searching large text journal databases. In order to remove ''search statements, record numbers, and system prompts,'' a special program is used to make search results uniform and easier for patrons to understand, even when the results are from different databases. The program automatically provides clearly labeled parts for each item in the search. Such results are easier to use and understand than the raw results from downloading. The program also checks citations against a library holdings database (by using the National Library of Medicine's unique number) to see if the journal is owned by the library. The journals holdings list was originally maintained on a campus mainframe but transferred to a PC for use with the database *STAR* with the NLM number added. Downloaded records are also sorted by journal to make look-up on the shelf easier. The BASIC software does a host of operations quickly on the downloaded record, including the adding of holdings records to the search results.

Significant Problems: None reported

Reference: None available

Project Date(s): January 1985

| | |
|---|---|
| Cost: | Not given |
| Self-Rating: | Not given |

| | |
|---|---|
| Name: | **DIALOG Searching with a Macintosh** |
| Library: | Merriam Center Library |
| Contact Person: | Edward J. Valauskas |
| Address/Phone: | 1313 E. 60th St., Chicago, IL 60637; (312) 947-2161 |
| Profile: | The Charles E. Merriam Library was established 50 years ago and serves a group of nonprofit organizations in Chicago's Hyde Park area, including the American Planning Association, American Public Works Association, students and faculty of the University of Chicago, and the general public. The collection contains over 50,000 monographs, 100,000 reports, 800 periodical titles, and 1,000 annual and irregular serials. |
| Hardware: | Originally used 512K enhanced Macintosh, 1200-baud US Robotics Courier modem; now uses Macintosh Plus and Courier modem, or Macintosh SE with 20-megabyte hard disk and 1200-baud Apple personal modem, ImageWriter II or LaserWriter Plus printers. |
| Software: | Originally *MacTerminal* (Apple Computers) because of familiarity; now uses Venture's *MicroPhone 1.1* (Software Ventures) and DIALOG templates. |
| Description: | Prior to the use of the Macintosh, the library used a Texas Instruments 300-baud terminal/printer to access DIALOG. Even though research staff permitted to access the system were given an automatic $25 per month credit, they rarely used it unless they were in severe need, since the system was slow and difficult to use. With the introduction of the Macintosh, searchers can do most of their own work, though the library staff still helps out as needed, processing requests for materials found as a result of the search. The Macintosh has been found to have a number of advantages over the old system: it is friendlier to use, staff time to help users has been cut by 50 percent, most printing can now be done on the library's own inhouse ImageWriter II or LaserWriter Plus, printing costs are cut by as much as 70 percent, and most results do not need to be printed out since they are saved on floppy diskettes (and can be printed out as needed and located using the *MacWrite* search feature). |
| Significant Problems: | It is recommended that a number of software packages be tried or tested before selecting a final one. |
| Reference: | Jenks, Dennis A. and Valauskas, Edward J. ''Macintosh- |

Mainframe Applications in a Special Library,'' *Apple Library Users Group Newsletter*, Oct. 1986, p.30.

Project Date(s): Summer 1986–Present

Costs: Original costs, $1,600; Current costs, $3,500 (excluding printers).

Self-Rating: 10

Name: **OCLC on a Macintosh**

Library: Merriam Center Library

Contact Person: Edward J. Valauskas

Address/Phone: 1313 E. 50th St., Chicago, IL 60637; (312) 947-2161

Profile: The Charles E. Merriam Library was established more than 50 years ago and serves a group of nonprofit organizations in Chicago's Hyde Park area, including the American Planning Association, American Public Works Association, students and faculty of the University of Chicago, and the general public. The collection contains over 50,000 monographs, 100,000 reports, 800 periodical titles, and 1,000 annual and irregular serials.

Hardware: Macintosh Plus, US Robotics Courier 1200-modem.

Software: *MicroPhone v. 1.1* (Software Ventures), for its ability to create scripts.

Description: Use of OCLC (Online Computer Library Center) has traditionally been for libraries with OCLC M300 terminals. This project was an effort to use the Macintosh computer for that function. While some adjustments had to be made (described below), the process of using a Mac has worked well. A number of reasons prompted its use: the library already used one and was familiar with the Mac for a variety of other functions in the library; the Mac could also be used for other telecommunications purposes (contacting local Chicago bulletin boards, DIALOG, and online catalogs); and since it was already part of the Merriam Library's *AppleTalk* network, it could send downloaded records to several different printers. Finally, the Mac and related hardware costs less than the corresponding OCLC hardware. Not every Apple is without a worm, however, and it is reported that the transmission speed of the Mac (with a 1200-baud modem) is slower than the OCLC dedicated lines (2400 to 9600 baud). Lower transmission speed means greater online time and higher costs. A more expensive modem would alleviate this difficulty.

Significant Problems: One major problem (as originally seen by the staff of Merriam) was the fact that OCLC uses an expanded set of

ASCII characters, some of which are not available on the Mac. Through experimentation with the Mac keyboard, some of the equivalents were found. Once this problem had been overcome, day-to-day operations began, and the use of the Mac significantly reduced Merriam Library's backlog of materials (the main function for the Mac and OCLC's combinations had been to assist in the cataloging of a pre-1986 backlog of 2,000 items, and recent 1986–87 materials). A hit rate of 78 percent was achieved.

Reference: Valauskas, Edward J. "Use of the Apple Macintosh to Access OCLC: A Preliminary Report." *Apple Library User's Group Newsletter*, Oct. 1987, p.57.

Project Date(s): Summer 1987

Cost: Funding through library budget. Hardware and software costs were approximately $1,500.

Self-Rating: 10

Name: **Search Statistics with *dBase III+***

Library: East Health Sciences Library

Contact Person: Susan C. Speer

Address/Phone: Carolina University, ECU School of Medicine, Greenville, NC 27858; (919) 551-2212

Profile: A staff of 36 maintains a collection of over 90,000 volumes and nearly 2,000 periodical subscriptions. Subject interests include allied health, correctional services, environment studies, medicine, nursing, and social work.

Hardware: IBM PC

Software: *dBase III+* (Ashton-Tate), because of staff expertise and already owned.

Description: This project was initiated to track search funds by providing a more accurate method of monitoring statistics. (The previous manual method was time-consuming and often inaccurate.) *dBase III+* provides reports on the number of searches and "calculates charges to departments and individuals and prints end-of-the-month invoices for users unassociated with the university but with standing accounts." An initial meeting took place between the head of reference and the systems librarian to determine what to include and how reports should be generated. Data integrity and control were also included in the initial plan. The *dBase* program is easy to operate and has a menu of four choices: data entry, monthly reports, invoice printing, and exit to *dBase III*. Formatted screens are used for data entry instead of the dBase "APEND" command. Reports generated each month include data by vendor, by purpose, and by librarian. The librarian report also contains turnaround time, cost, and "searches performed and charged to the library." Archival data is not kept (data is purged after one month), since the annual report is done by another department independently. Since the program can be modified, changes are made in order to accommodate different departments, which may require different information (or in a different format).

**Significant Problems:** None reported

**Reference:** Speer, Susan C. "Managing Online Search Statistics with dBase III +," *Information Technology and Libraries*, Sept. 1987, p.223.

**Project Date(s):** April 1, 1986–April 15, 1986

**Cost:** No additional costs to library

**Self-Rating:** 10

# Output Measures

Output measures help librarians determine how well they are achieving their goals of service. The problem with some of the measures is that they are time-consuming. The single entry in this category helps to take some of the drudgery out of the process.

Name: **Patron Count Analysis**

Library: Lucy Scribner Library

Contact Person: David H. Eyman

Address/Phone: Skidmore College, Saratoga Springs, NY 12866; (518) 584-5000 ext. 2223

Profile: Skidmore College has an enrollment of approximately 2,200 and a faculty of 180. The library staff of 33 includes 8 professionals. The library contains over 300,000 books and 1,392 periodical subscriptions.

Hardware: IBM PC XT

Software: *Lotus 1-2-3* (Lotus Development), selected because of availability.

Description: A more precise method of obtaining building-use statistics was required due to student requests for an increase in library hours. The traditional method of counting patrons (either electronically or with staff) at a single access point was deemed insufficient, and hence a method of sending someone around the library to count patrons was devised. This method described use in a very "area specific" way, and could be performed as often as staff availability and need dictated. Areas to be counted were divided according to floor only. The application of a spreadsheet to the data led to the creation of a "template," or form, that can be filled out online. Columns on the spreadsheet represent floors of the building, while rows represent "days." Since each day requires twenty rows, it is easy to page the spreadsheet up or down a window to reach the next day.

Each of the rows within a day represents a time, from 8:30 a.m. to 1:30 a.m. Analysis of the raw data can then be obtained by average use and peak use. Average building use is simply a collection of the daily summaries.

Significant Problems: None reported

Reference: Eyman, David H. "Analyzing Patron Count on a Microcomputer Spreadsheet," *Library Software Review*, Mar.–Apr. 1987, p.80.

Project Date(s): Ongoing

Cost: No special funding necessary. Costs absorbed by regular library budget.

Self-Rating: 7

# Public Access Microcomputers

Public access microcomputers are involved in a great many services that have been attempted or offered by libraries through the years. Some of these include walk-in computer-use service, electronic bulletin boards, public domain copy library, workshops, summer reading clubs, and a hardware and software lending collection. The most popular (and the easiest) is the walk-in project, though it is not without difficulties. Approximately 11 percent of all public libraries offer such a service, based upon a majority of surveys taken during the past ten years (though some surveys have put the total number of libraries offering public access at nearly 50 percent). Such a service requires extra attention by staff (even if not extra staff), storage, security, software and hardware selection, and maintenance, etc. The results, though, are enthusiastic. Perhaps the most difficult sort of public access is loaning hardware and software. Hardware is very expensive, prone to breaking, and requires the software as well. Software poses problems because it can be ruined without the library's knowledge, is difficult to replace or backup, and is expensive, to say nothing of potential copyright problems. The best course under such circumstances is the public domain copy library, discussed below, which solves most of these problems.

|  |  |
|---:|:---|
| Name: | **Walk-in Microcomputer Use** |
| Library: | Liverpool Public Library |
| Contact Person: | Jean Armour Polly |
| Address/Phone: | Tulip & Second Sts.; Liverpool, NY 13088; (315) 457-0310 |
| Profile: | Serves a population of just over 50,000. Annual circulation is over 330,000, and the library owns approximately 54,000 titles. |
| Hardware: | Apple IIe, 128K, Atari 1040ST, with one megabyte and 720 RAM, RGB color monitor, mouse, shared dot-matrix printer (this system also has a Casio CZ-230S synthesizer, TEAC dual stereo cassette deck); Panasonic Business Partner (IBM-compatible), 640K dual floppy drives, Macintosh Plus (2) with one-megabyte RAM, and internal 800K |

microfloppy disk drives, external 800K microfloppy disk drive, and mouse. Apple IIgs, with one-megabyte RAM, RGB color monitor, mouse, two 800K microfloppy disk drives, 5 1/4 floppy disk drive, ImageWriter II dot-matrix printer with color capability, CP/M card. Apple Laser-Writer Plus laser printer available. Many of the microcomputers are "Appletalked" (networked together to allow them to take advantage of different peripherals such as the LaserWriter printer). A CD-ROM drive is also projected for the next year.

Software: Liverpool does not recommend specific titles, but a list of software used successfully for public access may be found in Polly's *Apple Computers in Libraries, Volume 1* (Meckler, 1986).

Description: Liverpool's important project is different from most other public access projects in several ways. It has a long history (as such things go) and has shown remarkable development and upgrade throughout; it also has a wide diversity of microcomputer-related services available and perhaps the greatest number of different types of computers in one library. In fact, the computer area has developed into its own department complete with a head of microcomputer services, room attendant, and even computer pages. The services are nicely outlined in a continuing series of pamphlets and publications for the public. One way to combat some of the problems has been to locate the computers in locations separate from the other activity in the library. Software is cataloged, packaged, and stored in special containers. Originally, patrons were trained in groups, but after many people finally began to acquire micros at home, it was no longer necessary, and a ten-minute slide show in which the patron could validate him or herself replaced the thirty-minute class and was a big hit with patrons.

Significant Problems: None reported

Reference: Polly, Jean. *Essential Guide to Apple Computers in Libraries, Volume 1* (Meckler, 1986).

Project Date(s): 1981–Present

Cost: The library received a $25,000 grant from the state of New York in 1986 to vastly expand the project.

Self-Rating: 10

Name: **Public Access in a Tiny Branch Library**

Library: Maywood Public Library—Branch

Contact Person: Mary Fletcher

Address/Phone: 840 S. 17th Ave., Maywood, IL 60153; (312) 343-0508

Profile: This storefront branch library serves the southern end of the Maywood community.

Hardware: Commodore 64, color monitor, one disk drive.

Software: Approximately 50 educational programs.

Description: This project was envisioned as a means of enhancing branch service by providing a microcomputer and software for hands-on experience for neighborhood children. A Commodore was chosen because of its low price (there was only a small budget to work with). A major problem to solve was where to house a microcomputer in a one-room branch library without disrupting the other activities. This was done by putting the micro in part of the work-room where it could be monitored and closed off when not in use. Appointments are made by the half hour at the circulation desk. Software is kept in a locked cabinet near the computer. Neither the distribution of software nor the making of appointments has caused any undue nuisance. In more than two years, the machine has needed service only once. The children in the area enjoy the microcomputer a great deal, and it is usually booked up during the day (the library is only open between 1:00 p.m. and 5:30 p.m. Monday through Saturday).

Significant Problems: See above

Reference: None available

Project Date(s): 1985–Present

Cost: Library budget for hardware; state per capita grant for software.

Self-Rating: 10

Name: **Loaning Microcomputers**

Library: Memorial Hall Library

Contact Person: Nancy C. Jacobson

Address/Phone: Elm Square, Andover, MA 01810; (617) 475-6960

Profile: This library has an annual circulation in excess of 315,000, with holdings of approximately 168,000. It is the sub-regional headquarters for the Eastern Massachusetts Regional System.

Hardware: Panasonic Senior Partner, 128K, 16-bit CPU, IBM-compatible.

Software: Came with computer, see below.

Description: Loaning microcomputers to the public was decided upon after Memorial Hall Library staff discussed many of the problems associated with traditional public access (in-house) use of microcomputers with other librarians. The problem of staff making the time necessary to manage

such a project seemed formidable, and so it was determined that loaning hardware was a better strategy. Hardware was chosen on the theory that a computer without a
printer was useless for many adult activities, and it needs
to be portable and reasonably priced. After a year of
searching, the micro that seemed to meet all of these criteria was the Senior Partner by Panasonic. This full-fledged
microcomputer functions well for most major applications.
When finally obtained, it began to circulate for $15 per
three-day period (for patrons 18 years or older); $10 per
day overdue charges. Because of the difficulty in replacing
manuals, damage entails a $100 fee. Software made avail-
able to patrons included: word processing, budgeting,
accounting, reports, file generating, and creating graphs.
Software titles included *GW Basic*, *VisiCalc*, *DOS*, *Word-
Star*, *pfs:File*, *Report*, and *Graph*. The service was publi-
cized through a local newspaper in which the library has a
weekly column. There was little staff involvement for
patron training. Staff mostly learned how to check the
machine for damage upon return. It was repaired only once
in two years, and service fell under the original warranty.

| | |
|---|---|
| Significant Problems: | None reported |
| Reference: | Jacobson, Nancy. "Loaning Microcomputers to the Public," *Public Computing*, July/Aug. 1986, p.7. |
| Project Date(s): | Spring 1985 startup. |
| Cost: | Friends of the Library, $2,000. |
| Self-Rating: | 8 |
| Name: | **Loaning Software in a Special Library** |
| Library: | Apple Computers |
| Contact Person: | Monica Ertel |
| Address/Phone: | 10381 Bandley Dr., Mail Stop 8C, Cupertino, CA 95014; (408) 973-2552 |
| Profile: | The Apple library serves company employees and operates a Software Resource Center that circulates software. |
| Hardware: | Apple II+, IIe, IIc, IIgs, Macintosh 128K, 512K, Plus, SE, II, LISA. |
| Software: | Packages are purchased that are of interest to company employees and their work at Apple Computers. |
| Description: | Originally, a Software Resource Center had been set up to allow Apple employees to have access to software for evaluation purposes. Software use was limited to in-house library use because of concerns over potential copyright problems. Unfortunately, this led to underuse of the collection since few employees had time to spend during work |

hours, often in a building in which they did not work (the company is scattered about in different locations). The copyright concerns were eventually resolved, however, with the introduction of signs posted in the SRC warning against illegal copying. A release form that employees had to sign was also produced. Software was now thought of "the same way we thought of other library materials such as books. . . . " The release form states: "I agree to borrow 3rd party software for no more than three calendar days at a time. I understand that any software borrowed from the Apple Library is subject to recall at any time and I agree to return a recalled software package promptly. I also understand that all third party products are for evaluation and test purposes only and that I am not authorized to make copies." After a year of such circulation, all has gone well.

| | |
|---|---|
| Significant Problems: | See above |
| Reference: | Ertel, Monica. "Check It Out! How the Apple Library Deals with Circulating Software," *Public Computing*, July/Aug. 1986, p.5. |
| Project Date(s): | 1983–Present |
| Cost: | Part of library budget. |
| Self-Rating: | 9 |

| | |
|---|---|
| Name: | **Walk-in Public Access** |
| Library: | Parlin–Ingersoll Public Library |
| Contact Person: | Randy Wilson |
| Address/Phone: | 205 W. Chestnut, Canton, IL 61520; (309) 647-0064 |
| Profile: | Privately endowed library serving 14,000 residents and surrounding Fulton County. |
| Hardware: | Apple IIe's |
| Software: | Fifty titles of all types: for preschool (*Sticky Bear* [Xerox], etc.); adult (*DB Master* [Stoneware], etc., *AppleWorks* [Apple Computers], *Homeword Plus* [Sierra On-Line], *Trivia Fever*, and *PFS* [Software Publishing Corporation] series); and for staff use. Public software was selected for ease of use, documentation, and menu-driven features. |
| Description: | This public-access microcomputer project has been popular with patrons from the beginning. It also shows how staff can overcome numerous obstacles and meet patron requests on an ongoing basis. Before patrons were allowed to use the Apples, a one-hour workshop was required, including the tutorial *Apple Presents Apple*. Originally, approximately twenty people at once were trained on the basic fundamentals of computers, but this pace eventually |

proved difficult and ineffective since there was no hands-on experience involved. This method was soon changed to a two-hour workshop for adults taught by staff in which two people worked at each computer. Children who had previous knowledge of the computer and could demonstrate it, did not require the orientation. These new methods were more effective and speeded up the process considerably. The common question of "What do we do now?" was resolved on an ongoing basis with the introduction of numerous workshops on word processing, database management, and BASIC programming. Updates about this program continue to reflect the library's willingness to change and update the program according to the needs of the community.

Significant Problems: See above

Reference: Logsdon, Lori. "Public Access at the Parlin-Ingersoll Library," *Public Computing*, Jan./Feb. 1986, p.3.

Project Date(s): 1983–Present

Cost: Library budget

Self-Rating: 8

Name: **Public Domain Circulation**

Library: Maywood Public Library

Contact Person: Patrick R. Dewey

Address/Phone: 121 S. Fifth Ave., Maywood, IL 60153; (312) 343-1847

Profile: Maywood Public Library serves a community of approximately 28,000 residents, approximately 70 percent black, the remainder split between Hispanic and white. It has one branch library (storefront) and one main library.

Hardware: Apple IIe

Software: Fifty diskettes of public domain software.

Description: This simple project provides approximately fifty diskettes of public-domain software for patrons to copy and take home. The software takes less than a minute per disk to copy and provides a service for those patrons who own their own Apples. Disks may not be removed from the library. This system reduces the temptation by some patrons to illegally copy copyrighted materials. Since the diskettes are only copies of original diskettes that are kept in a safe place, the loss or damage to one during patron use causes virtually no difficulties. Since this disk collection was obtained from local user groups, there was almost no expense involved.

Significant Problems: None

Reference: None available

Project Date(s):   1986–Present
Cost:   Blank diskettes only
Self-Rating:   10

Name:   **Workshops and Seminars**
Library:   North–Pulaski Library
Contact Person:   Patrick R. Dewey
Address/Phone:   Maywood Public Library, 121 S. Fifth Ave., Maywood, IL 60153; (312) 343-1847
Profile:   North–Pulaski is a large storefront branch of the Chicago Public Library and serves a community of predominantly Hispanic patrons. It encompasses approximately 6,000 square feet and is situated along North Avenue in the North–Pulaski business district.
Hardware:   One Apple II+ with 64K, Epson MX-70 printer, Hayes 300 internal modem.
Software:   Several thousand individual titles (many minor) were available at the Personal Computer Center, but few were directly involved with the workshops. Students could work at their own pace on any titles between classes.
Description:   As part of the Personal Computer Center, beginning in 1981, a series of workshops were instituted on various aspects of microcomputer technology, including one for librarians and several for the general public. The most popular one involved word processing, consisting of a two-hour lecture/demo on the Apple, showing how several popular packages worked and how they could be of use. A local secretary who owned a micro and did word processing as an avocation volunteered to do the workshops for free. Each time about thirty to forty quite enthusiastic persons showed up. Another program that was tried with less success was the four-week crash course on the use of the microcomputer. While approximately thirty students were enthusiastic, it was difficult to provide any meaningful hands-on experience during the week, since this interfered with regular library user activity with the microcomputer. A final effort at a four-week class tackled assembly language, was also taught by a local author, himself a programmer in assembly language. The course went well, but the same problem with students finishing class assignments on the one computer recurred.
Significant Problems:   Not enough computer time for students to finish their class assignments. It is recommended that there be enough computers to allow for any type of class since students need

hands-on experience and require time to do their home-work.

Reference: None available

Project Date(s): 1981–83

Cost: Friends of the Chicago Public Library provided $4,360, but no additional funding was required for the classes or workshops.

Self-Rating: 10 (one-time workshops); 5 to 7 (for the classes).

Name: **Circulating Public Domain Software**

Library: Arlington Heights Memorial Library

Contact Person: Harvey Barfield

Address/Phone: 500 N. Dunton Ave., Arlington Heights, IL 60004; (312) 392-0100

Profile: Serves a community of some 66,000 people, with over 341,000 volumes and a staff of 39.

Hardware: Apple II+, IIe, IBM PC, Model 30.

Software: Software for Apple II models, Commodore, and IBM. Most software was purchased on the advice of patrons. IBM software was purchased through the PC-SIG users group.

Description: The library had been advised against circulating copy-righted software by their attorney because of the shrink-wrap laws in effect at that time. As an alternative, it was decided to build a collection of software without copy-right, i.e., public domain. Once a collection had been gath-ered from mostly free sources, procedures were devised that ensured a minimum of staff time and a minimum of lost software. Software is processed with Dewey numbers, there being thus far approximately fifty diskettes. Disks circulate for one week, with overdue fines of a dollar a day. A master set of diskettes is maintained as backup, with a circulating set used as boilerplate to create as many copies of a title as required. When diskettes are returned, staff need not check to see if they are okay; they need only note that a disk was returned, since all software is copied anew each time.

Significant Problems: Only with copyright already mentioned above. Public domain solves most handling and potential liability prob-lems.

Reference: None available

Project Date(s): 1986–Present

Cost: Normal library budget funds of approximately $500.

Self-Rating: 5

Name: **Macintosh Computers for Public Use**

Library: Torrance Public Library

Contact Person: Jacquelin Siegel

Address/Phone: 3301 Torrance Blvd., Torrance, CA 90503; (213) 618-5941

Profile: Serves a population of nearly 133,000 with an annual budget of $2.5 million. Holdings include 175,000 book titles and nearly 400,000 total volumes.

Hardware: Originally, the library owned a 128K Macintosh. This was finally upgraded to a Macintosh Plus.

Software: A variety of software is now available, though nearly all was given to the center by vendors as complimentary copies, since the center has no budget for acquisitions.

Description: The public access project of the Torrance Public Library featured both an IBM-compatible computer and a Macintosh. Both are in considerable demand, the IBM only slightly more than the Macintosh. There being no budget or staff assigned to the project specifically, everyone shares responsibility for the center as time allows. Use is by appointment. For security reasons, the machine is cabled and locked to the table; the keyboard and the mouse are both kept at the service desk. To use the center, patrons are required to attend an orientation session, during which a librarian explains the rules, the Macintosh and how to insert and use the diskettes, and what other services are available. To inform patrons on an ongoing basis, the library has prepared an excellent and useful "Microcomputer Center User's Guide and Information Package." Aside from the hardware and software lists, the guide contains the rules for those contemplating such a service. A "User Agreement" also spells out the responsibilities of the users and the terms guarding against potential damage (either to the Macintosh, the software, or to the user's data or diskettes).

Significant Problems: Finding a "guided tour" of the Mac and training patrons.

Reference: None available

Project Date(s): 1986–Present

Cost: A grant through the state originally purchased the Macintosh for adult literacy training purposes. After the two-year grant program expired, one Macintosh was placed out for the general public to use.

Self-Rating: None given

Name: **Microcomputer Center for Adults**

Library: Chester County Library

Contact Person: Marguerite Buck

Address/Phone: Chester County Library and District Center, 400 Exton Square Pky., Exton, PA 19341; (215) 363-0884

Profile: The County Library and District Center serves a population of over 300,000, with 16 member libraries.

Hardware: Five IBM PCs, each with printer.

Software: Eighty commercial packages, and 500 shareware and public domain programs.

Description: A genuine effort has been made to attract adults to this center and provide a wide range of services. Users must be 18 years or older (see grant restrictions below). The center provides use of microcomputers in the building, and also allows users to check-out software for home use. In addition, the Chester County Library plays host to a PC "users group" once a month. Library patrons have a chance to learn about many aspects of microcomputers through this club and its seven special interest groups. There is no cost to use any of the equipment or software, but there is a fee charged for expendables (5¢ per sheet of paper, 3¢ per sheet when using the patron's own paper, and 10¢ per sheet for graphics printing–*Print Shop*, etc.). Users must bring their own data disks. For persons without prior computer experience, a special orientation program is required, held twice each month. Appointments are not required, but they are recommended. A general disclaimer for the center reads: "The Chester County Library assumes no responsibility for any damage or loss of data, or any other consequential damage arising out of patron's use of the Library's hardware, software, or related facilities."

Significant Problems: None reported

Reference: None available

Project Date(s): Current

Cost: Originally funded from a grant "to be specifically used for *adult* computer education."

Self-Rating: Not given

# Reading Projects
# and Clubs

Reading clubs and microcomputers have functioned well together through the years. Some areas of the country have used it as a statewide theme, while some local libraries have actually set up a microcomputer and allowed children to input their own results as a way to spark interest in reading and curiosity about the computer.

| | |
|---:|:---|
| Name: | **Summer Reading Club** |
| Library: | Upland Public Library |
| Contact Persons: | Pat Castaneda and Marie Rooth |
| Address/Phone: | 450 N. Euclid Ave., Upland, CA 91786; (714) 981-1035 |
| Profile: | Serves a population of over 52,000 with nearly 100,000 volumes and 500 periodical subscriptions. A staff of 27 includes 4 professionals. |
| Hardware: | Apple IIes, one disk drive each, on loan each year from Upland School District. |
| Software: | BASIC programming by staff. |
| Description: | This project provides good ideas on interesting 600 kids to use the microcomputer (even if there are only four microcomputers). This was accomplished by making the micro a part of the summer reading club. Each young user picked up some basic computer skills, kept track of his or her own progress, and even registered without help. The program that was used to input data was created by the library staff in BASIC and took several hours. One advantage to this process is that the program does not "hide" what it is doing but displays each command as it executes it: accessing disk, writing file, and even defining some computer terms. The point of all this is to enhance the child's learning about the computer. Data were accessed by participant's access number, not name, simply because it was faster. Since so many children forgot their numbers, a printout was posted nearby. Considerable hand-holding for |

staff was initially required, but this eventually paid off when the library prepared for a fully automated system. The summer club used a Monopoly-like game board (designed by Marie Booth, children's librarian) for which moves were given for coming to library programs, playing trivia games, guessing book titles, etc. A special tilted ramp, down which a checker could be aimed and rolled, determined how many moves one would get each time (similar to rolling dice to get to move in real Monopoly). Children registered themselves on the computer for the club, and input their own scores (not book titles, since the scores were awarded for various activities) into the computer file. The computer is a peripheral but important part of the summer reading program.

Significant Problems:  Perhaps the greatest problem has been sort time for the program, requiring more than twenty-four hours when all 600 names have finally been input. Because of the volume of names, participants must be divided between computers and must use an assigned computer during the entire program. These problems have not been insurmountable, however, and the program is now in its fifth year. One suggested improvement is to connect all Apples or computers to a single hard-disk drive, both speeding access time and making it possible for a student to use any computer.

Reference:  Castaneda, Pat. "A Summer Reading Program," *Public Computing*, May/June 1986, p.2.

Project Date(s):  1984–Present

Cost:  No additional costs to library

Self-Rating:  8

# Reference

| | |
|---|---|
| Name: | **Automated Periodical Reference Service: Installing and Using Infotrac's** *Magazine Index* |
| Library: | Whitmore, Salt Lake County Library System |
| Contact Person: | David Ellefsen |
| Address/Phone: | 2197 E. 7000 South, Salt Lake City, UT 84121; (801) 943-4636 ext. 213 |
| Profile: | Serves a population of over 426,000 with an annual circulation of close to three million. Holdings include over 882,000 volumes and 589 periodical subscriptions. The system has fourteen branch libraries. |
| Hardware: | IBM PC (provided by Information Access), Canon Fax (model 510). |
| Software: | *Search Helper* (Information Access) |
| Description: | Salt Lake County Library System has implemented several new automated services within its fourteen branch libraries. In particular, *Search Helper* allows user-independent access to Infotrac's *Magazine Index*. The initial impetus for implementation of this system was one of cost; since patrons wanted access to the most current information, the library felt obligated to find a more economical means for them to obtain it. With the help of *Search Helper*, patrons set up a search strategy offline, and then automatically dial for them, search, gather the data, and log off. This fully automatic system allows even first-time, online users the opportunity to conduct their own search without library assistance. Seven hundred searches ($2.50 each) were paid for by the library in advance. Initially, the system was available only at the main library, but requests soon led to its installation in all branch libraries. With the use of *Magazine Collection*, another service from InfoTrac, many articles that appear in *Magazine Index* may be obtained full-text immediately, offline. The library staff feels that these |

products represents an 80 percent or more savings over the use of print and similar search tools.

Significant Problems:    None reported

Reference:    Ellefsen, David. "Automated Periodical Reference Service," *Information Technology and Libraries*, Dec. 1985, p.353.

Project Date(s):    1985–Present

Cost:    General library budget; cost was over $100,000.

Self-Rating:    10

Name:    **Local Table of Contents**

Library:    Health Science Library, University of Tennessee

Contact Person:    Lois M. Bellamy

Address/Phone:    877 Madison Ave., Rm. 248, University of Tennessee, Memphis, TN 38163; (901) 528-5155

Profile:    Serves nearly 800 faculty and 2,000 students.

Hardware:    IBM PC AT

Software:    *dBase III+* (Ashton-Tate), because of staff familiarity with it.

Description:    Providing a local table of contents service is superior to reliance on a commercially produced product such as *Current Contents*; it can be produced faster, be more specialized, and may perhaps be more economical. It can also be a lot of work, so Bellamy set out to automate the service when demand for tables of contents began to grow. The original manual system involved five distinct steps: (1) check in journals in Kardex; (2) lay aside journals flagged in Kardex for table of contents service; (3) consult list of table of contents service recipients (hospital staff had been surveyed to see who wanted to receive which tables of contents) for number of copies and patron names; (4) make photocopies; and (5) address and mail. The new system, which involves using *dBase*, is a set of programs designed by the library staff. Together, they automate the system into the following new set of steps: (1) make menu selection for journal check-in and enter journal issue information into a computer file; (2) make menu selection to run a program to produce a report of table of contents to be mailed (includes journal name, number of copies to make, and receipient's name and address); (3) make photocopies; and (4) affix computer-generated mailing labels. Clearly, the computer program is an advantage in several ways: it is no longer necessary for staff to spend time sorting out who gets what, and they no longer need to manually generate computer labels. The more patrons and the more journals that are being dealt with, the more efficient and useful such a program becomes.

Significant Problems: Potential developers of such a program are warned that programming in *dBase* (or in any command language) can be difficult and time-consuming without proper knowledge and experience.

Reference: Bellamy, Lois M. and Guyton, Joanne. ''Automation of a Local Table of Contents Service Using *dBase III*,'' *Library Software Review*, Sept.–Oct. 1987, p.253.

Project Date(s): February 1985–March 1985

Cost: Hardware and software also used for other library projects. No special grants. Total cost included purchase of IBM PC AT, *dBase III* +, and staff time.

Self-Rating: 9

Name: **Subject Guide Wall Chart**

Library: Maywood Public Library

Contact Person: Patrick R. Dewey

Address: 121 S. Fifth Ave., Maywood, IL 60153; (312) 343-1847

Profile: Maywood Public Library serves a community of approximately 28,000 residents, approximately 70 percent black, the remainder split between Hispanic and white. It has one branch library (storefront) and one main library.

Hardware: Apple IIe

Software: *Data Factory* (Microlab), now defunct, though any database system capable of sorting and handling at least 500 records will do the job.

Description: Prior to the advent of the microcomputer, creating anything but the simplest of wall charts was nearly impossible. Yet, with a micro, a sophisticated, comprehensive, and highly useful guide can be produced with a minimum of effort. The finished product, usually a laminated board approximately two by three feet (though they can be of any size desired), contains some 500 or more subject headings. Students and other patrons see the chart and immediately know how to use it, often saving the librarian much time spent answering simple routine questions that patrons should look up in the card catalog but don't. The mechanics of creation begin with simple note-taking as questions are asked by the public. This makes the chart highly specific for a particular library. Once sufficient entries have been identified (and they may be kept on scraps of paper, in notebooks, or in any other way), they are entered into an electronic database system, sorted, and a draft copy printed out. Fields for the database usually consist of only two or three: subject, LC number, or Dewey number. Once the text has been edited and any additional entries made, a printed final draft may be either laminated directly or taken to a typesetter (an especially good idea if the library does not have access to a laser or high-quality printer), and finally sent to a company that can make it into a sturdy sign ready for display. (Poster board that has been laminated will work just as well though not look quite as professional.) Staff may save from 10 to 50 percent of the time spent on simple everyday questions. It also makes a great browsing tool for students doing projects or term papers.

Significant Problems: None reported

Reference: Dewey, Patrick R. and Garber, Marvin. "Easy to Use Microcomputer Generated Subject Guide Wall Chart," *Online*, Mar. 1983.

Project Date(s): 1983–86

Cost: Library operating budget; cost per chart was approximately $100.

Self-Rating: 10

# Serials Control

Serials lists, especially long ones, can be difficult and extremely time-consuming to control. They often pose problems in routing to the proper departments, to check-in, or to budget. The project below shows one library's effort to convert a serials list of over 33,000 active and dead titles from a mainframe to a microcomputer format. See the special library circulation file on p.47 for an automated routing distribution system.

Name: **Serials Lists**

Library: Kansas State University Libraries

Contact Person: Charlene Grass

Address/Phone: Manhattan, KS 66506; (913) 532-7405

Profile: The university has an enrollment of over 18,000 and a faculty of 2,215. Total book collection exceeds 900,000 volumes, with 8,000 periodical subscriptions.

Hardware: Z386 (80386 microprocessor), 80-megabyte hard disk.

Software: *dBase III+* (Ashton-Tate), chosen for familiarity and functionality.

Description: The existing serials database that was maintained on a mainframe computer had to be converted for microcomputer use without reentering the data. This was done using mainframe data processing to divide the file into records and fields, since the original mainframe database had no true field divisions. Two lists are currently maintained on the library microcomputer. The first contains over 33,000 active and dead serial titles. The second contains only currently received titles. Each record is composed of the following fields: data of change to record; ISSN; OCLC number; title/description field; and call number. The title/description field is divided into (1) title; (2) summary holding information; and (3) specific location holding information. Lists are accessed through a common menu that allows for *dBase* editing of files with custom editing procedures. The finished product is a microfiche that is widely distributed at the university. Programs were written by University Computer Center, but new problems are solved by the library's microcomputer specialist.

Significant Problems: This type of project requires that the librarian be absolutely certain of various specifications and requirements. ''Insist on full technical documentation.'' Continuous training is also important for all involved.

Reference: None available

Project Date(s): 1986–Present

Cost: General operating funds, $5,000 for original hardware, software, and programming; $200 quarterly, ongoing.

Self-Rating: 7

Name: **Periodicals Management with *AppleWorks***

Library: Nepean Public Library

Contact Person: JoAnne Cybulski

Address/Phone: Nepean Civic Square Bldg., 101 Centrepoint Dr., Nepean Central Library, Nepean, Ontario, Canada K2G 5K7

Profile: Serves over 85,000 people with some 220,000 volumes. Annual circulation is over 850,000. Staff totals 97, including 11 professionals, 58 clerical, and 28 pages.

Hardware: Apple IIc, 128K, two disk drives, Zenith monitor, Apple printer.

Software: *AppleWorks* (Apple Computers), because of ease of use, inexpensive, and readily available.

Description: This project improves periodical management in the library in several ways, including better management of funds, cancellations, inventory, and an up-to-date holdings list. The library has approximately 438 active subscriptions. The database module of *AppleWorks* was used to design a database with eleven fields: title, type (location in collection, specifically adult, juvenile, newspaper, hi-tech, professional, index, and bookmobile collections), P/I/B (professional/index/bookmobile), REF/E (reference English), REF/F (reference French), CIRC/E (circulating English), CIRC/F (circulating French), vendor, estimated cost, actual cost, and remarks. Most of this is self-explanatory, but how some of the fields are used requires additional explanation. A ''1'' is used in each field for which a title qualifies, making it easy to total and identify collections. The first four types in the ''type'' field (adult, juvenile, newspaper, hi-tech) were all cross-referenced for language and collection category. For instance, a noncirculating juvenile magazine in French would not only receive a "juvenile" in the type category, but also a "1" in the REF/F field. Duplicate titles can also be placed in separate categories (if, for example, there is one circulating and one reference copy). The last three types (professional, index, and bookmobile collections) were only added to the P/I/B field since additional information (e.g., language break-down) was not needed. Vendor field shows from where a subscription is obtained: "C" for CANEBSCO or directly from the publisher ("D"). Actual price paid during the current budget year for a subscription was entered into the actual cost field, while unpaid subscriptions were entered into the estimated cost field, based on the previous year's cost. "Remarks" is a place for miscellaneous information, e.g., free, two subscriptions held, canceled, etc. Useful reports (using the program's report generator) include titles in a category, category cost, title grand total, and costs. These reports provide valuable information for collection analysis and future planning. A "Holdings List" was also generated using the basic database above. Using the three fields of "Title," "Type," and "Remarks," deleting all other fields, and adding the new fields of "Reference Printed," "Circulation Printed," and "Microform," an alphabetical listing by title and type was printed out as was an individual list for each collection. (Note: Though the "Remarks" field was retained, all of the information in that field was deleted and new information, such as in-house locations, title changes, etc., was entered.)

Significant Problems: None reported

Reference: None available

Project Date(s): 1985

Cost: No library costs

Self-Rating: 10

Name: **Periodicals Management Using a Macintosh**

Library: Merriam Center Library

Contact Person: Michael A. Wilson

Address/Phone: 1313 E. 60th St., Chicago, IL 60637; (312) 947-2162

Profile: The Charles E. Merriam Library was established more than 50 years ago and serves a group of nonprofit organizations in Chicago's Hyde Park area, including the American Planning Association, American Public Works Associa-tion, students and faculty of the University of Chicago, and the general public. The collection contains over 50,000 monographs, 100,000 reports, 800 periodical titles, and 1,000 annual and irregular serials.

Hardware: Originally used a Macintosh 512K-enhanced; now Macintosh SE with 20-megabyte internal hard disk.

Software: *Microsoft File* for ease of use and low cost.

Description: Periodical records were maintained as a paper file, but this became untenable as library patrons' need for an up-to-date listing of the library's holdings forced a decision to convert a computerized system. Using the *Microsoft File* program, a database management system, a database with the following fields (with length maximums in parentheses) was created: Title (138), ISSN (11), Publisher (138), Publ. Addr. (138), Zip Code (13), Freq. of Publ. (64), Subj. Heading (138), Subscr. Exp. (64), Price (64), Retention (64), Route List (138), Check In/Vol. (138), Notes (138), Source (138). All except the expiration field (date) and the price field (number) were created as text fields. Other fields that contained numbers, e.g., the Zip Code field, were formatted as text, because to format them as number fields would cause *File* to drop any initial zero. The "Source" field holds information about how the periodical is obtained (only 17 percent of some 800 periodicals are subscriptions). The field labeled "Retention" describes how long a periodical is to be held before being discarded, and therefore also identifies holdings. A number of reports can be generated conveniently by using *File*, including individual route lists for staff members, a master title list, and a monthly list to anticipate expirations.

Significant Problems: As of this writing, the library was still trying to devise a way in which a "Claims" field could be added to help identify missing issues. Presently, a "Check-in" field must be scanned instead.

Reference: Valauskas, Edward J. "Periodicals Management with the Macintosh in a Special Library," *Apple Library Users Group Newsletter*, Oct. 1986, p.25.

Project Date(s): February 1986–Present

Cost: Regular library operating budget, startup costs (hardware and software) $1,400.

Self-Rating: 7

# Student and Patron Assistance and Training

| | |
|---|---|
| Name: | **Résumé Preparation for Patrons** |
| Library: | Library/Learning Center, University of Wisconsin–Parkside, Kenosha, Wisconsin |
| Contact Person: | Linda Piele |
| Address/Phone: | P.O. Box 2000, Kenosha, WI 53141; (414) 553-2221 |
| Profile: | Serves 5,000 students with a variety of graduate and undergraduate programs. |
| Hardware: | Macintosh computers, Imagewriter printers, Laserwriter, and daisy-wheel printers. Macintosh is easy for novices to use. |
| Software: | *MacWrite* (Apple Computers) |
| Description: | Many students need to be able to prepare a good résumé but have no prior experience with computers. To accommodate them, the library began a hands-on workshop to teach format, content, and style skills. By doing this on the computer, they picked up another important skill—word processing. The workshop was a cooperative effort between the Library/Learning Center and the Career Planning and Placement Office. The Macintosh was chosen (the library has several different types of computers available) because of the visual representation of a document on the screen; students could have immediate feedback as they made change. Staff prepared a handout for how to get *MacWrite* started, and how to edit, save, and print documents. In addition, and prior to the workshop, students were given lists of do's and don'ts, samples and guidelines for résumé preparation, and a list of active verbs. A worksheet for résumé preparation is completed prior to the workshop itself, which gives the participant an opportunity to think about and gather the necessary information for a successful résumé. |

The workshops are divided into three sections. In the first part, students are introduced to material on "content, format, and styles of résumés," in a room separate from the microcomputers. The next part is hands-on and students are taught how to use the Macintosh. Basic skills such as inserting a disk, turning the machine on or off, etc., are demonstrated. In phase three, students begin using the skills they have learned so far to word-process their own résumés. As they gain skill in using the program, instructors teach them more and more advanced commands. It is obviously important to have someone skilled in both word processing and résumé preparation in order to make such a workshop a success.

Significant Problems: Classes should be kept small, and individual participants should not be counseled during the workshop. Groups should also have similar needs; mixing people with very different résumé types may lead to problems.

Reference: Nicholson, Donna. "MacResume: Teaching Résumé Preparation on a Microcomputer," *Public Computing*, Nov./Dec. 1986, p.2.

Project Date(s): January 1986–June 1987

Cost: Equipment already in place; no additional expense incurred. Blank data disks supplied during workshop. Other incidental costs: paper, transparencies, handouts, publicity.

Self-Rating: 9

Name: **Computer Fair Organizing**

Library: Brookens Library

Contact Person: Brian Alley

Address/Phone: Sangamon State University, Springfield, IL 62794; (217) 786-6597

Profile: Serves a student population of 3,450 and a faculty of 185. Approximate holdings are over 250,000 books and 3,200 periodical subscriptions.

Hardware: IBM, Compaq, Epson, NEC, Kyocera, Apple, Kaypro, Tandy, Commodore, and two local PC clone vendors.

Software: Some shareware exhibited.

Description: The computer fair has long been a way for users to "kick the tires" of their favorite computer models, according to Alley. This nonthreatening method of making hands-on experience available can be rewarding for all involved. As part of the university's Fall Festival, the computer fair attracted some 2,000 participants. Several planning sessions were essential, and invitations went out to many local computer vendors, including IBM, Compaq, Epson, NEC, Kyocera, Apple, Kaypro, Tandy, Commodore, and two local PC clone vendors. While there was little in the software line for this particular year, one vendor did demonstrate shareware; more software exhibits are planned for the future. There was no staff training involved and the only consultants were two who exhibited. Staff work included setting up the exhibit area, inviting the vendors, and seeing that power was provided for all of the machines. This small staff for help and security worked from 10:00 a.m. until 5:00 p.m.

Significant Problems: None reported

Reference: Alley, Brian. "The Do-It-Yourself Computer Fair: Planning, Pitfalls, and Payoff," *Small Computers in Libraries,* June 1988, p.6.

Project Date(s): October 1987–Present

Cost: Several hundred dollars to print and mail flyers.

Self-Rating: 10

Name: **Young Adult Career Guidance**

Library: Elmhurst Public Library

Contact Person: Mary Sue Brown

Address/Phone: Brown now works at the Woodridge Public Library, 3 Plaza Dr., Woodridge, IL 60517; (312) 964-7899

Profile: Serves a population of 44,000 with over 141,000 volumes. Annual circulation is approximately 400,000. Staff consists of 45, including 10 professionals.

Hardware: IBM PC XT, printer, color monitor.

Software: *System of Interactive Guidance and Testing* (SIGI) (Educational Testing Service).

Description: The goals for this project were twofold: to help students who were unsure of career orientation to "discover their interests"; to locate specific career information. This was to be done through a software package called *System of Interactive Guidance and Testing*, and through a series of appropriate subject bibliographies. Catering in particular to the high school dropout, the career programs were presented to groups of eighty or more, and reached a total of 500 young adults through special promotional activities. At least five patrons per week used SIGI. Evaluations by more than 300 participants were nearly 100 percent positive. Some consulting was done through the Suburban Library System Consulting Services, with the additional help of Jim Lauer, professor of computer science at Northern Illinois University. Planning of the project took fifteen hours, though staff orientation to the software only required ten minutes.

SIGI has a series of subsystems that deserve some comment. The first is an introduction that explains the concept behind the program, helping students to decide what they need to do next. Users then make an exploration of ten occupational values and are asked to rate their importance (e.g., satisfaction desired, trade-offs, etc.). In "Values and Occupations," students choose five values at a time and rate their importance to create lists of appropriate occupations. Information is supplied about occupations according to and related to various values and occupational ratings. Finally, occupations are examined in light of possible rewards they offer versus risks of entry into that occupation.

Significant Problems: Few problems presented themselves. Staff reported the process as "painless."

Reference: None available

Project Date(s): April 1, 1984–September 30, 1984

Cost: LSCA funding of $5,000; local Elmhurst Public Library funding of $1,650.

Self-Rating: 10 for SIGI; 8 for total project

Name: **Computerized Career and Information Center**

Library: Maywood Public Library/Broadview Public Library

Contact Person: Patrick R. Dewey

Address/Phone: 121 S. Fifth Ave., Maywood, IL 60153; (312) 343-1847

Profile: A cooperative project of two small public libraries whose communities adjoin.

Hardware: IBM PC, two disk drives, dot matrix printer.

Software: Not yet purchased, but a variety of software to assist students in their efforts to find a job was located for consideration. This software would help improve taking tests and locating appropriate college and financial assistance.

Description: Because of high dropout rate in area schools, this project was conceived to assist students in several ways. Continuing their education to make their job skills more marketable was paramount, but improving scores on college tests, succeeding with the GED, and finding the right college and financial assistance were also considered crucial. Libraries would provide the use of the microcomputer, software, and staff assistance for students. Each high school, and many local community organizations, would be contacted in order to make the site and its opportunities known. (For fuller discussion, see appendix A, Sample Project Proposal, at the end of this book.)

Significant Problems: Report not yet available

Reference: None available

Project Date(s): Spring 1988

Cost: Approximately $5,000 per library.

Self-Rating: Not given

Name: **CD-ROM Electronic Encyclopedia**

Library: Surrattsville High School

Contact Person: Brenda Karnes

Address/Phone: 6101 Garden Dr., Surrattsville High School Library Media Center, Clinton, MD 20735; (301) 868-0653

Profile: Surrattsville High School teaches grades 9 through 12, with a student population of nearly 1,300

Hardware: IBM PC System 30, Hitachi drive, Apple II with Hitachi CD-ROM, Jonathan Card.

Software: Comes with CD-ROM using *Knowledge Retrieval System* software unique to this system (won't work with other CD-ROM setups).

Description: CD-ROM offers several significant advantages over traditional storage devices. It can, first of all, be thought of as merely another form of disk, used with a special disk drive. Unlike traditional hard-disk drives, CD-ROM is perhaps more reliable (less subject to data destruction in the event of a breakdown), will hold vast amounts of data even when compared to hard disk drives (as many as 200,000 typed pages or 500 megabytes of data storage), and it is, through a combination of laser and microcomputer technology, amazingly simple to search data. This project was envisioned as a research project for determining how CD-ROM could assist a high school library. Grolier's *Academic American Encyclopedia* was chosen as the subject for the research. This database is the equivalent of the twenty-volume, 30,000-entry encyclopedia online, requiring sixty megabytes of storage space. The *Knowledge Retrieval System* software allows searching in two modes: browse entry (title search), and word-search mode, which permits full-text searching of the database. Once an article that looks interesting has been located it is a simple matter for the student to call it up.

A variety of issues became apparent to staff as they planned for and worked with this new technology: standardization, configuration, access, security, and cost. The problems of standardization meant that software (used with the micro to retrieve data from the CD) is different for each database. This often requires either a row of machines dedicated one to each database or that the microcomputer software and the CD be changed for each database. If the system is public access, this can cause problems and damage. Furthermore, each system requires that the user learn a new system for searching.

Configuration considerations mean that care must be taken to ensure that the proper interface boards, operating system, and other factors be given ample attention, especially since such purchases are expensive.

The library must decide whether or not the public will have access to the equipment. If not, the library staff must provide the expertise and time necessary to provide the service.

Security of the equipment is a vital issue, since a CD is a small, pocket-sized disc that can be carried away easily. Special locking devices for the players can be installed, but that means dedicating the machine to a particular database.

The results of this experiment have been considered spectacular by those involved.

Significant Problems: It is recommended that libraries proceed slowly, since not all new technologies work out as first expected.

Reference: Barlow, Diane; Karnes, Brenda; and Marchionini, Gary. "CD-ROM in a High School Library Media Center," *School Library Journal*, Nov. 1987, p.LC66.

Project Date(s): 1987–Present

Cost: Major funding from Central Media Services, some equipment (hardware) on loan from University of Maryland, and remainder provided in-house.

Self-Rating: 7.5

Name: **End-User Searching with CompuVend**

Library: Hagerty Library

Contact Person: Tim LaBorie

Address/Phone: Drexel University, 32d and Chestnut Sts., Philadelphia, PA 19144; (215) 895-2794

Profile: The library serves over 10,000 students and 457 faculty. Number of volumes exceeds 400,000.

Hardware: Macintosh Plus

Software: *MacTerminal* (Apple Computers), enhanced and renamed *DUTalk*. *MacTerminal* is licensed to the Drexel campus, available to students, and is simple to use.

Description: CompuVend was chosen as a method for reducing the amount of time necessary for staff to assist student patrons searching an online system. It also provides password protection and collects funds. This arrangement does not provide for complete independence for students: they must be trained to some extent and occasional help is required to get them through the search. But the system's automatic log-on and other features provide for a considerable reduction in staff time and many students, once oriented, can proceed on their own. The end-user search station is located near the reference desk and is available whenever there is staff at the desk. Staff loan the software and assist when necessary.

Significant Problems: Time required to keep up with system changes in order to provide good documentation to users.

Reference: LaBorie, Tim and Donnelly, Leslie. "Planning for End User Searching: Drexel and the Mac—A User Consistent Interface," ED26877; LaBorie, Tim and Donnelly, Leslie. "Vending Database Searching with Public Access Terminals," *Library Hi Tech*, June 1986, p.7–10.

Project Date(s): January 1984–Present

Cost: A grant to the university for the hardware. Lease of CompuVend is recommended (rather than purchase).

Self-Rating: 8

Name: **Literacy**

Library: Haydon Burns Library, Jacksonville Public Libraries

Contact Person: Jean Brinkman

Address/Phone: 122 N. Ocean St., Jacksonville, FL 32202; (906) 630-2426

Profile: Serves a population of over 600,000 with some 400,000 volumes and 11 branch libraries. Annual circulation approaches two million. The staff of 117 includes 51 professionals.

Hardware: The CAL lab has six Apple IIe computers. Two have two disk drives and one has an Epson FX80 printer. There is also available a 512K Macintosh with an Imagewriter printer. One of the Apple IIe's also uses an ECHO+ speech synthesizer.

Software: A variety of user-friendly software, appropriate for adults reading at third- to sixth-grade level was selected to promote or improve literacy.

Description: This project combined microcomputer technology with a literacy program for functionally illiterate adults aged 16 and up. It attempts to teach basic reading, consumer math, and other basic life skills. The target group was students reading at a third- to sixth-grade level. Computer technology was seen positively because it provides disadvantaged students with math, spelling, reading, and other basic skills. It also provides these skills in ''1) a non-threatening environment, 2) individualized instruction, 3) positive reinforcement, 4) the computer always responds to the student . . . , 5) improved self-esteem stemming from the student's use of the computers, 6) increased self-confidence from being in control, 7) ability to repeat drill and practice exercises as many times as needed to learn a skill, and 8) none of the negative connotations of the typical classroom setting in which most of these students had only experienced failure.'' Student applicants are interviewed and tested for reading level. Once accepted, a flexible schedule is set up for one, two, or three sessions per week, one or two hours per session. Individualized learning plans are devised for each student. Student enrollment in the program is approximately 25 to 30 at a time. According to the center, some 540 individuals have been interviewed and evaluated since April 1985. The program has three full-time paid professionals, including a coordinator and two assistants. Participants are either referred to the center from the local Laubauch Literacy Action Agency, or from other groups and agencies, or respond to public service announcements on television.

Significant Problems: None reported
Reference: None available
Project Date(s): 1984–Present
Cost: LSCA grant of $60,000 first year; decreasing to $25,000, fourth and final year. Other sources of support have been found in order to continue the program.
Self-Rating: 10

# Systems

| | |
|---|---|
| Name: | **In-House Integrated Library System** |
| Library: | DALIS Automated Systems (Defense Communications Agency Library) |
| Contact Person: | Margaret Martinez |
| Address/Phone: | 9007 Lee Highway, Fairfax, VA 22031; (703) 692-2468 |
| Profile: | Not available |
| Hardware: | M300 (IBM PC), 640K, 20-megabyte hard disk |
| Software: | *dBase III* (Ashton-Tate), since it was already owned and staff knew how to use it. Any similar database management system should work, though. |
| Description: | The project was conceived to reduce staff time in library operations in many areas; in short, to be a total library system, that would, in turn, increase staff involvement with patrons. The system provides for acquisitions and circulation (including reserves, serials control, online catalog, and reference subsystem). The programming was done in-house and involved basically one program, *dBase III*. There was considerable staff time spent in the planning stages, including a feasibility study, system analysis, and system design. New staff orientation requires very little time since the system is completely menu-driven and easy to use. Use of such a system— i.e., in-house programming using a command structured database—is recommended by the people involved in this project only if the staff expertise and time are available and access to other, larger computers and more costly, fully developed software is not available. It is also recommended that the collection size be less than 15,000. |
| Significant Problems: | Newer and more powerful versions of *dBase* are recommended by staff as is access to programs such as *Quicksilver* (WordTech Systems) or *Clipper* (Nantucket). These |

programs reduce the time required to create a *dBase* program.

Reference: M300 and PC Report, July/Aug. 1986, p.1–5.

Project Date(s): January 1986

Cost: No additional costs incurred

Self-Rating: 10

Name: **Multi-Campus Library Automation**

Library: Hillsborough Community College

Contact Person: Viveca Yoshikawa

Address/Phone: 1502 E. 9th Ave., Library Bldg., Rm. 304, Tampa, FL 33605

Profile: This four-campus college library has special collections in art, business, and music, book and nonprint. Book titles number approximately 60,000.

Hardware: Three IBM PC XTs with 30-megabyte hard disk, laser disk drives, and RS-232 controller cards, with VAX access, a DEC VAX 11/780 mini-computer, VT220 and Ditto 221XL terminals, and laser barcode scanners.

Software: *BiblioFile Catalog Production System* (The Library Corporation), used to convert collection for *Ocelot Library System* (Aball Software).

Description: The Accreditation Committee, Southern Association of Colleges, recommended that the union catalog of the holdings of the four campus libraries be microfilmed and made available at all campus sites. Instead, the library decided to generate machine-readable records, making use and access to catalog records more efficient. An automation committee was formed and began an extensive investigation for hardware and software. Only $20,000 was available for the project. Some of the specific goals and objectives for the project were: (1) master union list must be accessible at all four campuses; (2) each campus must be able to automate circulation; and (3) all must be able to tie into local and state systems (MARC record format therefore essential). Software was needed for both retroconversion and current cataloging, database searches, and circulation. The college's in-house computer center provided some advice and assistance in the selection of software and the use of existing hardware. Extensive staff training was required, and only one staff member was computer literate. Training consisted of both hands-on workshops and seminars. Seven staff were involved in retrospective conversion, two doing initial data input, three specializing in different areas, and one supervising. The library has purchased three separate *Ocelot* modules: *Catalogue*, *Circulation*, and *Purchase*. Records are accepted by *Catalogue* from the *BiblioFile* system, which converts them to the *Ocelot* format and database as full MARC records. In the Public Access Catalog, patrons can search by author, subject, title, or classification number (Boolean and cross-reference searching as well). *Circulation* supports "all standard circulation functions," including checking in or out, reserves, renewals, overdue notices, etc. The *Purchase* acquisitions module will handle up to 15,000 orders per year. The decision was made to use *BiblioFile* first for conversion, then set up the *Ocelot* system. For two months the conversion process continued, and it speeded up as staff grew more skilled.

Significant Problems: Generally pleased with *Ocelot*, though some minor problems exist, which programmers are currently trying to solve. It is recommended by the project staff that if more than one software package is used, they should be completely compatible. One specific technical problem: *BiblioFile* did not generate records exactly as *Ocelot* required. Fortunately, only 2,500 records had been entered when a test of the system discovered the problem, and corrections were made with only two weeks lost.

Reference: None available

Project Date(s): Summer 1985–Present

Cost: Grants

Self-Rating: 9

Name: **Integrated Library System**

Library: Methodist Hospitals of Memphis, Leslie M. Stratton Nursing Library

Contact Person: Denise Fesmire

Address/Phone: 251 S. Claybrook, Memphis, TN 38104; (901) 726-8862

Profile: The Stratton library staff consists of one professional and one student assistant. The collection is mainly medical science with approximately 1,000 book titles. Book volumes and bound periodicals total over 5,000.

Hardware: IBM AT with 20-megabyte hard disk, 1.2 megabyte floppy.

Software: *Sydney Micro Library System* (Sydney Dataproducts), selected based on recommendations from users of the Sydney minicomputer system and because of discounted purchase price from pre-release purchase.

Description: Increased circulation of materials forced library to consider an online system. All staff members at this library were involved in the planning of the total project. Installation took nearly a year. Staff members attended DOS and *dBase* workshops and learned word processing, all of which proved useful when it came to the retrospective conversion of records. The system includes three modules: cataloging/inquiry, circulation, and MARC interface. The cataloging/inquiry function permits maintenance of the database: add/modify catalog, authority, and inventory data; barcode linking, inquiry, and print reports. Reports that can be generated include labels (batch or individual), bibliographies, catalogs, inventory reports, and authority term reports. Most of the library's holdings, however, already existed on tape at Marcive and were sent to Sydney for conversion to floppy disks and finally copied to the library's hard disk. It took seven months to process or enter 6,000 records, at which point the library circulation system went online. More than 600 active patrons were entered into the computer and their cards typed and barcoded. During retrospective record entry and editing, the MARC interface was unable to retrieve records from Marcive. Now that this phase is complete, catalog records are being retrieved online from Marcive.

Significant Problems: Preplanning is stressed, though it is impossible to forecast all of the changes that will be required once the system is online. Also, having a single-user system rather than a network originally created problems. For instance, since the system is chiefly for circulation, all activities must be performed at the circulation desk. As of December 1987, however, the Sydney system was finally networked so that the circulation staff had full use of one terminal. Future plans call for the purchase of the acquisitions module, but not the serials module, since the library uses *dBase III+* for handling their small collection of 106 serials.

Reference: None available

Project Date(s): Planning began July 1984; online, August 1986

Cost: $15,000, library capital budget

Self-Rating: 8

Name: **Model Library Utilizing Microcomputers**

Library: MMI Preparatory School

Contact Person: Nancy Everhart

Address/Phone: 154 Centre St., Freeland, PA 18224; (717) 636-1108

Profile: School library serving 200 students. Holdings consist of approximately 9,000 books, 2,000 AV items, and 100 magazine subscriptions. A certified media specialist and a library clerk are included in the staff.

Hardware:  Thirteen Apple IIs, one Profile hard drive, four printers, one Tandy 1200 HD, two CD-ROM disk drives, printer.

Software:  *Circulation Plus* (Follett), *Quick Card* (Follett), *Apple-Works* (Apple Computers), 200 educational programs, and others (see below).

Description:  This excellent project shows how to apply microcomputer technology in a comprehensive way to the library environment. With the assistance of a technology grant, the library concentrated its efforts on fifteen areas of computerization: catalog card production, online reference, circulation, word processing, graphics, hardware circulation, software circulation, software and hardware evaluation, provision of computer reference materials, library skills instruction, interlibrary loan, bibliography generation, administrative use of databases, training teachers, and training students. A few notes about some of these areas are in order.

*Quick Card* is used for catalog card production. With this program, a job that used to take a clerk eighteen hours, now requires two hours (for forty books). Information, once entered into this database, can also be dumped into the *Circulation Plus* database without further keying-in of data. The online reference notation above refers to a subscription to BRS (Bibliographic Reference Service) and the ability to search the more local Pennsylvania State University's online catalog, LIAS. The full-text articles that are referenced by BRS citations may be searched in the library's collection. LIAS materials may be ordered through regular interlibrary loan. In addition, the library provides access to Guidance Information System (GIS), an online service that lets students search for appropriate colleges by location, tuition, major, and other factors. Word processing is performed with the *Bank Street Writer* (Broderbund) as well as *AppleWorks*, and is used for thank-you letters, news releases, long-overdues, etc. *The Print Shop* (Broderbund) and *The Newsroom* (Springboard) are used for signs, bookmarks, note paper, banners, book plates, and the library newsletter. Create with *Garfield* (DLM) is used for custom disk labels and cartoon signs. The circulation of software has caused no undue problems; documentation is photocopied for backup purposes, the package laminated, and barcodes used to enter it into the circulation system. Only Apple II programs are available. The library also makes three Apple II computers available for circulation (monitors not included), and they are for overnight loan only. Parents must sign a responsibility statement (for damages) prior to circulation. During the first year, there was no damage to any of the computers. Part of the grant money was used for other materials, such as computer books for students and faculty, and for additional reference materials for the media center. *Bibliography Writer* (Follett) is used to generate easily revised book lists. Workshops for teachers have introduced them to the growing use of computers in the school. Computer classes are held regularly for students.

Significant Problems: None reported

Reference: "Library Project Is Winner," *Apple Library Users Group Newsletter*, Oct. 1987, p.52; "Model Electronic Library," *Small Computers in Libraries*, Mar. 1986, p. 10; "Model Library Utilizing Microcomputers," in *Check This Out: Library Program Models* (U.S. Department of Education, 1987), p.91; "Library Resource Sharing," *Media and Methods*, Nov./Dec. 1986, p.10.

Project Date(s): September 1985–Present

Cost: Chapter II grant for $28,647

Self-Rating: 9

Name: **Inventory and Union List of Libraries**

Library: Northwestern Regional Library

Contact Person: Joyce Latham

Address/Phone: 111 N. Front St., Elkin, NC 28676; (919) 835-4894

Profile: This library serves ten member libraries and has a circulation of nearly 400,000 volumes and owns over 200,000 volumes.

Hardware: IBM AT

Software: *dBase III+* (Ashton-Tate), selected because of its ability to handle large database and staff familiarity with program.

Description: The RegionBook database project automated the acquisitions of thirty years (48,000 books) in a system library, ultimately compiling a union list of holdings in member libraries that circulate or rotate from library to library. Technical services for these libraries are centralized. Only with the advent of low-cost computers and programs such as *dBase III+* has it been possible for the system to create an accurate union list of region-owned books that circulate throughout the system. Materials had been tracked in what was called the "blue card file," but this was not considered very reliable for interlibrary loan. In fact, the collection, prior to this project, had never before been inventoried. The database is available on floppy disk to libraries that own computers, or as a printout for those that do not.

| | |
|---|---|
| Significant Problems: | Suggestions included the use of a hard drive and a faster computer and software. *dBase* was found to be slow when using more than one index, and queries are difficult. |
| Reference: | None available |
| Project Date(s): | July 1987–Present |
| Cost: | Funded by Regional Board. Computer purchased from LSCA allocation by state; software from AV line item, and current staff used for inputting/searching. Total cost about $4,000 (hardware is used for other projects, not a single function). |
| Self-Rating: | 8 |

# User's Network

Name: **Microaide User's Network**

Library: Library, Department of Finance/Treasury Board of Canada

Contact Person: Frank White

Address/Phone: 140 O'Connor St., Ottawa, Ontario, Canada K1A 0G5; (613) 995-6076

Profile: Contains over 80,000 volumes and 1,600 periodical subscriptions. Nineteen staff members provide and maintain special-interest collections on accounting and auditing, business and management, economics, finance, government programs, industrial relations, and more.

Hardware: IBM PC, 640K, 20-megabyte hard drive, printer.

Software: *Edibase* (Personal Library Systems), a text-based management package with bilingual capabilities that are important because of official French and English languages in the area. The package also has stronger indexing capabilities than *dBase* (Ashton-Tate) software.

Description: The finished product of this project is a hard copy directory of microcomputer information concerning 320 federal government libraries in Canada. According to Frank White, chairman of the project, "Information sharing among a network of users could accelerate the learning process and improve the quality of decision making." Membership is by application. Invitations to join the network were sent to 320 federal government libraries in Canada. The Task Group, headed by White, was made up of Eric Clyde, Rick Harkin, Barry Jensen, Margo Jeske, and Barney Shum. This hardbound directory of information contains headings in both French and in English. Data is arranged alphabetically by Canadian library symbol, with each entry containing sections on hardware, software, and applications (with software cross-reference), comprising 71 pages in length. Indexes are by library name, software, and library application. Based on survey results, the Task Group will eventually look into the possibility of setting up an electronic bulletin board system to enhance the user-group characteristic, though at this writing there is no online version for members to access.

Significant Problems: None reported

Reference: Alsford, Stephen, and White, Frank. "Edibase," *Library Software Review*, July/Aug. 1987, p.210.

Project Date(s): 1987–Present

Cost: National Library of Canada funded several hundred dollars in printing costs. Labor was donated.

Self-Rating: 8

# Miscellany

There are many hundreds, if not thousands, of library tasks that can be computerized, only a few of which can be discussed within this section. Staff training, creating a user group, and the streamlining of any repetitive task are certainly worthy projects and can be applied to many different types of situations. The other projects listed here simply do not fit neatly into any of the above categories.

Name: **Training Staff with a Microcomputer**

Library: University of Florida Libraries

Contact Person: Suzanne J. Shaw

Address/Phone: Systems Office, Library West, Gainesville, FL 32611; (904) 392-0796

Profile: The University of Florida Libraries contain more than 2,250,000 book volumes and bound periodicals. It is divided into a number of departmental libraries.

Hardware: IBM PC, 128K, one disk drive, or M300.

Software: PC BASIC package consists of one 5 1/4-inch floppy disk, information manual, "cheat sheet," and M300 guidelines.

Description: One of the hardest tasks associated with installation of a microcomputer in the library is the training of staff. Some personnel are just not interested, and training can be time-consuming under any circumstance. Most of the library orientation software that exists does not address staff training, but it can teach patron skills, e.g., how to use the card catalog, how to locate a book on the shelf, etc. This project sought to train staff using an application programmed by staff themselves. In this case, *How to Search OCLC* was the technique used. The staff not only uses the in-house software effectively, but also has fun, since the exercises are designed as a game. The program is self-paced and draws a series of drill and practice exercises from a large body of examples, making each session different. All of the practice concerns searching and covers such details as

''Mc/Mac rule'' and the ''Stoplist.'' Four one-hour lessons are part of the package. The materials are considered useful for student assistants and clerical staff in technical services, new professionals for orientation, undergraduate and graduate students in library science, and for the general public in some cases.

Significant Problems: No significant problems were reported, but it was suggested that such a project requires lots of testing.

Reference: An excellent brochure further describing the software and program is available from the contact person listed above.

Project Date(s): 1984–85

Cost: Release time for author and student programmer was only cost incurred.

Self-Rating: 10

Name: **Creating a Library User Group**

Library: Grosse Pointe Public Library

Contact Person: Blaine V. Morrow

Address/Phone: 10 Kercheval, Grosse Pointe, MI 48236; (313) 343-2340

Profile: Serves a population of more than 58,000 with 120,000 volumes, 14 professional and 18 clerical staff.

Hardware: All microcomputers and peripherals.

Software: All types of software used in libraries.

Description: This project grew out of the realization that ''many local librarians were beginning to use microcomputers and needed help, advice, training, etc.'' and represents a group of libraries that formed the Librarians Using Computers (LUC) users group. The general purpose is to provide a way to share information about computers among members. Some of the potential output of such a group includes newsletters, meetings, product reviews, group discount purchases, and even workshops. Membership (fees provided below) is open to librarians using any brand microcomputer or software. Some of the specific functions that the group performs include reviewing ''good and bad, expensive and cheap, easy and nearly impossible'' software, provide outside speakers, and quarterly (or more often) meetings at which products are reviewed with hands-on experience and public domain software can be exchanged. Some of the advice offered by potential leaders has included ''avoid trying to force directions on the group; let them take you where they want to go.'' Some tips for setting up shop include: maintain a good and active board of directors; plan meaningful programs; provide good leadership and affiliate with other user groups.

Significant Problems: See project description above
Reference: None available at time of publication.
Project Date(s): October 1984–Present
Cost: Individual memberships of $5 per year. Institutional memberships of $10 per year.
Self Rating: 10

Name: **Service for Faculty (Checkoutable Micro)**
Library: Pennsylvania State University
Contact Person: Michael W. Loder
Address/Phone: Schuylkill Campus/Penn State Campus Library, Box 308, Rte. 61, South, Schuylkill Haven, PA 17972; (717) 385-4500
Profile: The Schuylkill campus has an enrollment of approximately 700 freshmen and sophmore students. About 90 live in the dormitory; the rest commute. There are 35 full-time and several part-time instructors.
Hardware: Apple IIc, Apple monitor, Apple modem.
Software: *AppleTerm* is easy to operate. *AppleWorks* (Apple Computers) added because of popularity.
Description: LIAS (Library Information Access System), Penn State's online catalog system, which offers access to the main collections at University Park and other Commonwealth campuses, became available at Schuylkill in February 1984. The problem was to make this database available to everyone at the campus. According to the library's own 1987 survey, only three of the faculty owned modems, and only 30 percent owned a micro of any kind. The solution was to purchase an Apple IIc (nearly all other micros on campus at that time were Apples) with carrying case, monitor, modem, and printer. Equipment and *AppleTerm* communications package were offered to faculty on an "as-needed" basis. Announcements were made at a faculty meeting and flyers placed in mailboxes. A remote demonstration was also given during the first week of the spring semester. Faculty finally requested the machine, but often for purposes other than the original intention of remote searching (most often for word processing). Offering such a special service to the faculty also "stimulated use of other services." As a result, the library did find a way to spur involvement with microcomputers and produce good public relations as well.
Significant Problems: If project were started anew, "I would get a Macintosh and appropriate software such as *Red Ryder* (Freesoft) or *MacTerminal* (Apple Computers). The Mac proved to be

just as transportable if not more so, and requires no computer skills to operate.'' There were no significant problems of hardware or software failure and no faculty complaints. Ultimately, 25 percent of the faculty used the micro but only about 3 percent for its original purpose.

Reference: Loder, Michael W. ''Remote Searching an Online Catalog Using Checkoutable Microcomputers,'' *Library Software Review*, Jan./Feb. 1988, p.3

Project Date(s): June 1984–June 1986

Cost: A grant from university funds for faculty research in the amount of $2,177.

Self Rating: 9

Name: **Streamlining Repetitive Tasks**

Library: Texas Tech University Library

Contact Person: Pat Marx

Address/Phone: Lubbock, TX 79409; (806) 742-2245

Library Profile: Serves 25,000 students with over 2 million books.

Hardware: IBM-compatible

Software: Written in-house

Description This project automated several distinct tasks at the library: bindery slip preparation (including label manufacture), printing call numbers from downloaded OCLC information, and staff time sheets. These tend to be tasks that require the same data to be entered over and over again. For instance, the bindery slip program generates multiple copies and inserts data as required by commercial binders. Labels were printed from the OCLC call number using software produced in-house, and a font program was used to generate call numbers on labels in a larger size. Time sheets (submitted every two weeks) were filled in using commercial software. Both math and other basic data were entered this way.

Significant Problems: None reported

Reference: Marx, Patricia. ''Use of Microcomputers to Streamline Repetitive Processing Tasks,'' in *SCIL 1988 Conference Proceedings* (Meckler, 1988), p.67.

Project Date(s): 1984–Present

Cost: Software was free

Self Rating: 9.5

Name: **Sheet Music Index**

Library: Music Library

Contact Person: Nancy F. Carter

Address/Phone: University of Colorado, Boulder, CO 80309; (303) 492-3928

Library Profile: Houses one of the largest music research collections in the United States. 40,000 scores and 20,000 volumes of books and periodicals.

Hardware: Radio Shack, Model II

Software: *Profile* file maintenance program was available at no cost and filled needs.

Description: This project organized 2,000 scattered sheets of old popular music, a potential source of information and use by patrons. Previous efforts to index the material manually failed because of lack of time and personnel. Though not warranting individual OCLC cataloging, multiple access points were deemed to be important. In order to plan the database, input was solicited from current and former library staff and faculty. The actual project was handled by a staff member who specializes in such projects. Organizing the music for data entry was problematic, and meetings took under consideration what kinds of data fields should be established: first line, era, composer, etc. It was finally decided that the music should be arranged alphabetically on the shelves by year. Additional access (by computer) was determined to be: first line, title, and composer. Finding all of the music turned out to be a scavenger hunt, with sheets hidden in unusual places. Vocal music was the only kind retained, in English or with English translation. Incomplete music was discarded. To avoid confusion, the earliest year of copyright or published date was written at the top, and an assignment was made for citing composer and lyricist, when possible. The project required no computer programming, and in just a few hours it was off and running. The bulk of the remaining time was spent inputting data. Title, composer's last name, lyricist's last name, and first line were all used to generate indexes. Space considerations also required that the collection be divided logically by diskette, using six diskettes, each covering a different decade or era and containing 300 to 400 records. An input work sheet was created to speed data entry. Though satisfactory as originally conceived, the project ultimately ran out of room and was transferred to a mainframe.

Significant Problems: The software package had limited record length (132), which, once fields were assigned, allowed little room for comment.

Reference: Carter, Nancy F. "Sheet Music Index on a Microcomputer," *Information Technology and Libraries*, Mar. 1983, p.52; update: "Sheet Music Index at the University of Colorado: II," *Information Technology and Libraries*, June 1988, p.198.

Project Date(s): 1982–Present

Cost: Staff time only required

Self-Rating: 7

Name: **Statewide Referral Database: Indiana Youth Resources Information Network**

Library: Indiana Cooperative Library Services Authority (INCOLSA)

Contact Person: Becki Whitaker

Address/Phone: 5929 Lakeside Blvd., Indianapolis, IN 46276; (317) 298-6570

Profile: This network is comprised of 14 public libraries and 190 other Indiana institutions.

Hardware: Each library has a local area network (LAN) with Televideo hard-disk drive, two IBM-compatible workstations, Bernoulli box, and modem. The network information is distributed through the Bernoulli box via removable hard-disk cartridges. Locally stored information is sent to the state database every six months for merging, while the complete database is sent to each participant in the same way.

Software: Developed as a menu-driven system by INCOLSA using *dBase III+* (Ashton-Tate) and *Clipper*, a compiler.

Description: Several problems had to be solved in order to make this project work. First, there was the collection of data for community resources. Then it was necessary to have the data from the fifteen participating libraries merged into a single database and redistributed to each as a complete file. This also had to be done periodically, as information needed to be updated. An independent consultant was hired who made recommendations about most areas of the project. The record format was standardized and the same software database and hardware were used at each site. Every six months the new collection of data records is sent by cartridge to a central site, merged, and returned. Data were collected from questionnaires sent to each agency, which would be included in the database. The actual record itself contains thirty-one fields. While it is in many ways a centralized process, end-user libraries have much control over the system. *Thesaurus of ERIC Descriptors* was decided upon as the vocabulary authority for the database. A Quality Control Committee is responsible for handling problems regarding standardization and policy development.

Significant Problems: None reported

Reference: None available

Project Date(s): 1985–Present

Cost: Initial funding derived from a grant from the Indiana Criminal Justice Institute (July 1985)

Self-Rating: Still in development

Name: **Cataloging Sound Recordings**

Library: Iowa State University, Music Listening Room, Department of Music

Contact Person: Dawn E. Work

Address/Phone: Work may be contacted at the Public Library of Des Moines, 100 Locust St., Des Moines, IA 50308

Profile: Departmental listening library with a large number of sound recordings and sheet music.

Hardware: Apple IIe, two disk drives, Okidata dot-matrix printer.

Software: *Cards* (Addison Public Library, highly recommended).

Description: The *Cards* program was used to catalog lengthy sound recording data which, if cataloged manually, would have been entirely too costly. The program allows for 256 characters per field, formats according to AACR2 standards, and prints cards in any number, with extra analytical and added entries.

Significant Problems: None reported

Reference: *Apple Library Users Group Newsletter*, Apr. 1986, p.14.

Project Date(s): 1985–86 school year

Cost: Not given

Self-Rating: Not given

# Sample Project Proposal

## Maywood/Broadview Mini-Grant Proposal

A Computerized Career and Education Information Center (CCEIC) will be located at the Maywood Public Library and the Broadview Public Library and will provide a variety of information and educational software, which will assist the young adults who have either dropped out of high school or who have difficulty in selecting or preparing for a career, employment, or college. There are six distinct areas of need: (1) choosing a career; (2) choosing an educational institution that will help to fulfill the requirements of the career; (3) finding financial assistance; (4) preparing for educational testing (SAT, ACT, etc.); (5) obtaining a high school diploma through the GED; and (6) preparing a résumé. Each CCEIC site will provide a comprehensive plan for students:

Orientation to the computer and available materials
Interactive career guidance
Computer-assisted instruction for college testing
Computer-assisted college search program using a variety of variables
Computer-guided résumé preparation
Books and other materials related to the overall program (including college catalogs and printed career materials)
Locations and telephone numbers to obtain additional counseling for career guidance, GED test centers, etc.

Students will work at their own pace during one- or two-hour appointments and will have trained staff to assist in the use of the computer and software programs.

In addition, each site will provide bibliographies of related materials in each area, and provide permanent, professionally trained staff able to assist students with the fundamentals of computer and computer software operation (both sites currently have public-access microcomputers). Books and other materials, such as college catalogs, GED test site locations, and assistance books will be made conveniently available at each site.

Part of the project will involve the selection of software in each of the five computer areas described above.

# Need

Proper and adequate career and college counseling is not always available to high school students or dropouts. The high schools in the Broadview and Maywood communities have particularly high dropout rates. It is assumed that this plays some role in the high unemployment rate in the area (11.5 percent). The CCEIC will help the library to continue its traditional role as a repository for many types of resource materials, which have attempted to fill community need, in this case career and employment problems.

The computer age has made a variety of new approaches available. Using software that explains career possibilities, career requirements, colleges and other educational requirements, opportunities, costs, and many other related factors, young adults will be able to search for and learn about the many choices available to them. Finally, they will be able to improve their skills for taking college tests and find help in preparing résumés—both areas in which libraries have helped. Added to the library, the CCEIC will be one component in the overall development of available resources.

# Long-Range Plan

The project would help to fulfill the long-range goals and plans of the Illinois State Library and the Broadview and Maywood Public Libraries: to improve service to young adults because of their "special needs." These libraries have had a number of classes and workshops, both independently and in cooperation with local colleges (e.g., Triton), to assist the development and career opportunities of young adults. This new program will make available interactive computer resources in major areas of need.

# Goals and Measurable Objectives

Establish a Computerized Career and Education Information Center (CCEIC) at each participating library. This entails the following objectives:

Purchase of hardware
Selecting software in each area of activity
    résumé preparation
    career focus

college and educational possibilities and selection

college testing assistance (SAT, ACT)

GED-related programs

An introductory fact sheet about CCEIC will be created and distributed to each participant. This will outline rules, software available, what participants should be able to achieve with the materials, and where to go for additional assistance.

Staff orientation by Patrick Dewey

Creation of guidelines for use of centers as well as establishment of procedures and physical placement and handling of hardware and software

Prepare an evaluation form

Contact and schedule visits for local high school personnel and youth leaders. Though it is difficult to estimate, the centers would be expected to assist 500 patrons per year (minimum), which is less than 2 per day, to a potential of approximately 1,200 (or about 4 per day). Each use would be either walk-in or by appointment, depending upon availability. All use would be for two hours each, maximum.

Contact local unemployment offices

Promotional activities (newspaper, cable TV, etc.) for attracting young adults to the center

Making the center available for forty hours (minimum) each week

Incorporating the program into the overall strategy for reaching young adults by including it in publicity releases to newspapers, local schools, unemployment centers, etc.

Incorporating the program into a regular biennial feature of the library's overall strategy, including budgeting money for additional software updates on an annual basis.

Keeping statistics on how many students use the centers, and provide evaluation forms for each to attempt to determine how helpful the information has been and how best to improve the service.

# Evaluation will be by:

Record of phone calls about center and their origin

Random survey of guidance counselors at end of program from both public and private schools

Evaluation forms from people using centers

Numbers of people actually attracted to the centers

Evaluations from high school and other personnel who attend orientations or who refer people to the centers, and provide evaluation forms for each to attempt to determine how helpful the information has been and how best to improve the service.

# Budget

Equipment:
   one IBM-compatible computer with two disk drives,
      color monitors for each site              $ 2,816.00
   one printer for each site                    900.00
Software:
   one set for each site                      5,200.00
Supplies:
   paper, diskettes, ribbons                 530.00
Printing and publicity costs:              400.00

Total                                $ 9,846.00

Local libraries will provide staff time, tables, chairs, other physical facilities, and repair of equipment.

# Continuation Plan

The local libraries will continue the program on an ongoing basis after the original grant period expires and will continue to provide updates and enhancements to the software collection.

# Vendor List

**Aaron/Smith Associates, Inc.**
Suite 518
1422 West Peachtree St., N.W.
Atlanta, GA

**Aball Software**
2268 Osler St.
Regina, Saskatchewan, Canada S4P
1W8

**Addison Public Library**
235 N. Kennedy Dr.
Addison, IL 60101

**Aldus Corp.**
411 1st Ave. South
Suite 200
Seattle, WA 98104

**Apple Computer, Inc.**
20650 Valley Green Dr.
Cupertino, CA 95014

**Artic Technologies**
1311 N. Main
Clawson, MI 48017

**Ashton-Tate**
20101 Hamilton Ave.
Torrance, CA 90502

**Berkeley Systems Designs, Inc.**
1708 Shattuck Ave.
Berkeley, CA 94709

**Bill Blue**
Marilla Corp.
1274 Del Monte Dr.
El Cajon, CA 92020

**Broderbund Software**
Box 12947
San Rafael, CA 94913

**CE Software**
801 73d St.
Des Moines, IA 50312

**Computer Aids**
Box 1074
Vienna, VA 22180

**Computer Associates Micro Products**
Division
2195 Fortune Dr.
San Jose, CA 95131

**Condor Computer Corp.**
2051 South State St.
Ann Arbor, MI 48104

**Cuadra Associates, Inc.**
2001 Wilshire Blvd.
Santa Monica, CA 90403

**Data Trek, Inc.**
621 Second St.
Encinitas, CA 92024

**DLM (Development Learning Materials)**
1-DLM Park
Allen, TX 75002

**Dubl-Click Software**
18201 Gresham St.
Northridge, CA 91325

**Embar Information Associates**
1234 Folkstone Ct.
Wheaton, IL 60187

**Follett Software Co.**
4506 Northwest Hwy.
Crystal Lake, IL 60014

**Freesoft Co.**
10828 Lacklink
St. Louis, MO 63114

**Funk Software, Inc.**
222 3rd St.
Cambridge, MA 02142

**FYI, Inc.**
Box 26481
Austin, TX 78755

**Information Access Co.**
11 Davis Dr.
Belmont, CA 94002

**Innovative Software**
9300 W. 110th St., Suite 380
Overland Park, KS 66210

**KNM Systems Corp.**
6034 W. Courtyard Dr.
Austin, TX 78735

**Leading Edge Software Products, Inc.**
21 Highland Circle
Needham Heights, MA 02194

**Letraset USA**
40 Eisenhower Dr.
Paramus, NJ 07653

**The Library Corp.**
Box 40035
Washington, DC 20016

**Lifetree Software, Inc.**
411 Pacific St., Suite 315
Monterey, CA 93940

**Lotus Development Corp.**
55 Cambridge Pkwy.
Cambridge, MA 02142

**Micro Data Products, Inc.**
5739 S. Olathe Ct.
Aurora, CO 80015

**MicroPro**
33 San Pablo Ave.
San Rafael, CA 94903

**Microsoft Corp.**
16011 N.E. 36th Way
Box 97017
Redmond, WA 98073

**Microtech Consulting Co.**
206 Angie Dr.
Box 521
Cedar Falls, IA 50613

**Nantucket**
12555 W. Jefferson Blvd.
Los Angeles, CA 90066

**Nashoba Systems, Inc.**
175 Sudbury Rd.
Concord, MA 01742

**Novell, Inc.**
1170 N. Industrial Park Dr.
Orem, UT 84057

**PC-SIG**
1030D E. Duane Ave.
Sunnyvale, CA 94086

**Personal Library Systems**
Suite 912
7910 Woodmont Ave.
Bethesda, MD 20814

**Radio Shack**
(Contact local Radio Shack)

**Raised Dot Computing, Inc.**
408 S. Baldwin St.
Madison, WI 53703

**RoseSoft**
4710 N.E. University Way
Suite 601
Seattle, WA 98105

**Scarecrow Press, Inc.**
52 Liberty St.
Metuchen, NJ 08840

**Sierra On-Line, Inc.**
Box 485
Coarsegold, CA 93614

**Small Library Computing, Inc.**
48 Lawrence Ave.
Holbrook, NY 11741

**SoftLogic Solutions, Inc.**
530 Chestnut St.
Manchester, NH 03101

**The Software Group**
Northway Ten Executive Park
Ballston Lake, NY 12019

**Software Publishing Corp.**
1901 Landings Dr.
Mountain View, CA 94043

**Software Ventures**
2907 Claremont Ave.
Suite 220
Berkeley, CA 94705

**Sorcim**
2310 Lundy Ave.
San Jose, CA 95131

**Spectrum HoloByte, Inc.**
1050 Walnut
Suite 325
Boulder, CO 80302

**Springboard Software, Inc.**
7807 Creekridge Circle
Minneapolis, MN 55435

**Stoneware, Inc.**
50 Belvedere St.
San Rafael, CA 94901

**Sydney Dataproducts, Inc.**
11075 Santa Monica Blvd.
Suite 100
Los Angeles, CA 90025

**T/Maker**
1973 Landings Dr.
Mt. View, CA 94043

**Winnebago Software Co.**
109 W. Main Street
Caledonia, MN 55921

**WordPerfect Corp.**
1555 N. Technology Way
Orem, UT 84057

**WordTech Systems, Inc.**
Box 1747
Orinda, CA 94563

**Xerox Educational Publications**
Computer Software Division
245 Long Hill Rd.
Middletown, CT 06457

# Glossary of 101 Important Terms

Accoustic Coupler—A telecommunications device that converts digital computer signals to analog telephone signals using a telephone handset instead of direct connect wiring. More error prone than direct connect.

Analog—The continuous wave signal used by the telephone line. A pattern is determined based on changes in the signal. (Opposite of digital, which generates a series of separate [discrete] signals in the form of *1*s and *0*s.)

ASCII—American Standard Code for Information Interchange, an agreed-upon standard of 128 letters and other symbols. Each symbol is represented by a set of seven digits (*1*s and *0*s).

Assembler—A computer programming language that makes it possible for humans to interface with, or create, machine language programs.

Backup—A second or additional copy on a disk of a program or data.

BASIC—Beginner's All-Purpose Symbolic Instruction Code, originally created as a teaching language, but eventually gaining a following as an important high-level computer language.

Batch—Multiple instructions or data executed as a group, often typed from the keyboard (especially when used as a macro).

Baud—Shorthand for, "bits per second transmitted." Typically, data speed is 300 baud (300 bits per second), 1200, 2400, 9600, etc. Since each computer character requires some 10 bits each (including stop, start, etc., bits), this amounts to 30, 120, 240, etc., characters per second.

Bell Compatible—Both 103 Bell compatible and 212A Bell compatible refer to Bell Telephone standards. 103 refers to 300 baud and 212A refers to 1200 baud. Some modems are referred to as 103/212A or 300/1200 baud.

Bit—The smallest unit of information that a computer can process, either a *1* or a **0**. Bits are combined into groups of eight or more to form a *byte* (computer word).

Boot—The process of starting up a computer, preparing it for service. Usually, a small "bootstrap" program is loaded-in automatically, making it possible to then load other programs. A cold boot is performed when the power to the unit is first turned on, a warm boot if the machine is already on but needs to be "reset" for some reason.

Buffer—A space in memory reserved for a special function, such as a storage place for material being printed, saved from screen, etc.

Bulletin Board System (BBS)—An interactive, online database, which may have a number of features, including multiple lines in, upload/download of public domain and shareware programs, electronic mail, conference areas, etc. Usually, though not always, operated on a local microcomputer. Some BBS operate on national networks such as The Source or CompuServe.

Bundled—Software that comes with the hardware is ''bundled'' with the hardware. Often such a system includes a word processor and a database management system. The purpose is to make the system more marketable.

Byte—Generally, eight bits used during transmission, though stop and start bits may make it ten bits. A byte is basically a computer word (character) such as *W* or *1*.

CAI—Computer Assisted Instruction defines a lot of areas, but it includes any program that attempts to teach a skill through computer training.

CD-ROM—Compact Disk—Read Only Memory, a recently introduced storage device that differs in several important ways from conventional disk drives. CD-ROM will hold several hundred megabytes of data, and it is more difficult to damage or erase. A major problem with CD-ROM is that data on it cannot be erased. The WORM (Write Once, Read Many) is an effort to overcome this deficiency.

Central Processing Unit (CPU)—The central brain or processor of the computer, where timing, routing of data, and other decisions are made.

Chip—The basic hardware unit of microcomputer technology, made of silicon.

Circuit Board—A board that contains a number of chips and controls a device such as a printer or modem, or houses the RAM and ROM (memory) of the computer.

Clone—A computer that emulates a more popular name-brand machine in order to capitalize upon the market.

Command Language—An English-like computer language used with programs such as dBase to produce more sophisticated programs.

Compatible—See *clone*, above.

Compiler—A program that takes a BASIC or other high-level language program and converts it into the machine code of the computer.

Co-processor—A second or additional central processing unit in a computer.

CP/M Operating System—Control Program for Microprocessors was one of the first and most popular of the operating systems available for microcomputers. A large body of public-domain software contributed to its popularity.

Crash—A total, and usually sudden, system failure.

CRT—Cathode Ray Tube, referring to the monitor or TV screen used for computer program display.

Cursor—Usually a flashing square pointing to where the next character on the computer screen will appear.

Dedicated—Describes a program, telephone line, or other device used for a single purpose or function.

Default—Factory settings, hardware or software, which typically take over when the computer operator fails to make a conscious decision.

Desktop Publishing—Creating camera-ready copy with the computer and printer, often entailing a laser printer for high-quality reproduction, but also refers to simpler products produced on a dot-matrix printer and programs such as The Print Shop.

Digital—*1*s and *0*s that are combined into bytes to form computer words or characters, as opposed to the analog, or continuous signal, of the telephone lines.

DIP Switch—Dual In-Line Package, or the set of switches on a computer device that allows for flexibility permitting the device to be used with a variety of computers.

This is important because most manufacturers do not know what kind of computer their product will be used with later.

Disk Drive—The mass storage device that reads and writes to a disk. These data storage devices come in many sizes and types and may be built-in or external to the computer.

Disk Operating System (DOS)—The master control program that manages the filing system and interfaces with the disk drives.

Diskette—A small circular object to which data is stored and from which it is retrieved; used in a disk drive.

Documentation—The printed or online manuals that give the instructions for use of a program.

Download—To receive a program into a computer from a (usually) remote or distant computer. Opposite of *upload*. The program can then be copied to disk for future use.

Duplex—Can be either half or full duplex. *Full duplex* is simultaneous transmission in both directions, whereas *half duplex* is transmission in either direction but only one direction at a time.

Electronic Mail (E-Mail)—Sending messages electronically. May be done locally through a bulletin board system (BBS) or nationally through a nationwide network.

Encryption—A system for encoding data in a secret way as to prevent its retrieval or use by another party.

Ergonomics—The comfort (or lack thereof) provided in the workstation, including seating, lighting, and climate.

Error Message—Any message from the computer signal that something is wrong. Example: "Disk full."

Export Data—To move data from one program to another.

Font—Typeface.

Format—To "initialize" a disk for use by the computer.

Generic Software—Software not created for dedicated use but for a wide variety of uses. Includes word processors, database managers, spreadsheets, etc. Opposite of a program that, for example, creates catalog cards exclusively.

Graphics Tablet—An input device that allows the user to draw or trace objects that are then digitized for computer use.

Hacker—Though originally a term used to describe a computer enthusiast, it now implies someone who uses a computer for destructive purposes, such as crashing bulletin boards, invading mainframes illegally, or other mischievous acts.

Hard Copy—Printed computer data.

Hardware—The nuts-and-bolts parts of the computer that can be seen and felt, such as monitor, chips, keyboard, or disk drives.

Housekeeping—Maintenance programs or activities designed to keep a system up to working specifications.

Import Data—Reverse of *export*. To receive data from another program into your program.

Integrated Software—Software that does more that one thing, usually word processing, database management, spreadsheet, telecommunications, and graphics.

Interactive—Computer programs that require a human response. Non-interactive software (demo programs, for instance) will run without human intervention.

Interactive Fiction—Role-playing adventure games where the player takes the part of a character.

Joystick—The hand-held stick used for computer games and (sometimes as a menu control device).

Local Area Network (LAN)—A system that connects computers for the sharing of data, files, electronic mail, and expensive peripherals.

Mainframe Computer—A large computer usually requiring a special, climate-controlled room and support (hence the term *mainframe*, which refers to this support).

Memory—To a large extent, a computer's memory determines its Memory is its ability to store and hold data. Data may be stored internally in the computer's chips, or externally, on hard- or floppy-disk drives.

Microcomputer—A small desktop or home computer. The distinctions between the different sizes of computers blurs more each year as the large ones decrease in size and the small ones increase in power.

Minicomputer—A computer of medium range in both capability and memory.

Modem—From the terms *modulator/demodulator*, a device for translating the digital code of the computer into the analog code of the telephone line and back again. Two modems (one at each end) are required for two computers to communicate over the telephone. Computers can be directly connected without modems if they are close enough.

Monitor—The screen that displays the computer's answers or data.

Mother Board—The main circuit board to which all other circuit boards are connected. It houses the *RAM*, *ROM*, and *CPU*.

Multiplexing—A state in which a computer appears to be doing two things at once, but is really doing two or more things alternately but very quickly.

Off-the-Shelf Software—Software written for a very specific use and is not modifiable to any great extent.

Parallel Transmission—Data being sent eight bits simultaneously.

Parameter—A state such as baud rate, parity, line feeds, etc., which determines how a device or computer will act. These may be changed by the operator under software control or, sometimes, under hardware control with DIP switches, but parameter's always have factory settings (defaults).

Parity—A method for checking the accuracy of data transmission by adding up the data bits, which must be either odd or even. If the proper addition is not made by the computer, the data are rejected and retransmitted.

Peripheral—Any device not part of the computer proper, whether internal or external to the computer housing. Such devices include modems, printers, disk drives, and graphics tablets.

Printer—A device for printing out hard-copy computer results. Dot matrix, daisy-wheel, and laser are the most common types.

Protocol—An agreed-upon method for data transmission, which reduces the chance for error. For instance, if both computers "know" that all incoming sets of data or signals must add up to an even number, one coming in as an odd number is judged to incorrect and must be retransmitted (see *parity* above).

Public Domain—Software without copyright restrictions.

RAMworks—A memory card for the Apple computer that adds large amounts of internal RAM memory to the system.

Random Access Memory (RAM)—Memory in a computer that changes as the computer uses it.

Read Only Memory (ROM)—Memory that already has a program stored on it. The computer can read this memory or stored information, but it cannot change or add to it.

RS-232-C—A standard determining the interface between modems and computers.

Sector—A magnetically created rectangular area on a disk used by the computer to store, locate, and retrieve data.

Serial Transmission—Data being sent between computers one bit at a time in single file.

Shareware—Copyrighted software that is freely distributed. However, if the user wishes to continue to use it, a license fee must be remitted to the owner of the software (stipulated in the software itself).

Soft Copy—Information appearing on the computer screen, distinct from that which is printed out.

Software—The set of invisible instructions that tells the hardware what to do with the data it receives.

Source Code—Uncompiled program code that may be altered by users for their own purpose.

Spooler—A method of sending data to a buffer or storage area in order to free up the computer or other device. For instance, by sending a long file to a buffer, the computer may continue to function without waiting; by sending a second file to the print buffer, a line or queue is formed waiting for the printer to finish.

Spreadsheet—The electronic version of the accountant's pad. Formulas and data may be entered and the results calculated immediately. A second set of data or a change in any data element will result in a recalculation of the entire spreadsheet, making it possible to judge the effect of changes, for example, in budgets, very quickly.

Supercomputer—The most powerful computer in existence at a given time in history.

Surge Protector—A device that reduces harmful, momentary increases in electrical energy that is detrimental to computers.

Sysop—System Operator who controls, or has responsibility for maintenance of, a computer system, either micro-, mini-, or mainframe.

Synchronous—Data transmission that is regulated by synchronized clocks in both the sending and receiving computers.

Telecommunication—To communicate over long distances, through telephone lines, satellite, or other means.

Telecommute—Working at a computer terminal without having to physically go to the workplace.

Template—A form, electronic or paper, that represents work that someone has prepared, but that may be used over and over with different sets of data. An example would be a spreadsheet in which formulas have been placed for creating a budget. For example, any two businesses using the same kind of budget can use the same formulas.

Terminal—A place where users may interface with a computer, in the form of a key-board, a monitor, or a printer. The computer need not be present but is reached through either the telephone lines with a modem or directly through cable (known as *hardwiring*) in a local area network.

Track—Concentric magnetic rings on a computer disk, which, when divided into sec-tors, map out where data is stored on the disk. All diskettes come blank and must be formatted or initialized, a process that divides them into these magnetic tracks and sectors.

Upload—To send data to another computer. Opposite of *download.*

User Group—Any group of persons who get together for the purpose of exchanging information about computers, especially problem-solving. Such groups may host special events such as lectures or hardware/software demonstrations, or they may obtain group discounts on computers and supplies.

Word Processing—A software program that allows users to rearrange and revise text (sentences, words, etc.), without having to retype all data before hard copy is produced. These programs often come with "spellers," which check documents for (usually) misspelled words.

Workstation—An area that contains the necessary equipment (furniture, outlets, table, etc.) to work with a computer. The station where a person works on a computer. Such areas should have good lighting and comfortable seating (see *ergonomics*, above).

WORM (Write-Once-Read-Many)—A type of CD-ROM that allows for writing to disk but that cannot be erased and can be read as often as desired.

# Bibliography of
# Library Software
# Applications

For additional information on library use of microcomputers and software, consult the following publications.

Clark, Philip. *Microcomputer Spreadsheet Models for Libraries*. American Library Association, 1985. Presents models for many types of library work, including 57 specific models. Text was written for use with *SuperCalc2*, though the models may be readily adapted for use with other spreadsheets.

Costa, Betty and Costa, Marie. *A Micro Handbook for Small Libraries and Media Centers*. 2d ed. Libraries Unlimited, 1986. Covers the library use of microcomputers, plus provides many references for additional information. Includes many pertinent forms.

Desmarais, Norman. *Essential Guide to the Library IBM PC: Volume 11, Acquisitions Systems for Libraries*. Meckler, 1988. Reviewed are many of the major acquisitions packages currently on the market: *ACQ350, Any-Book, BaTaSYSTEMS Acquisitions, Card Datalog Acquisitions Module, MATSS: Midwest Automated Technical Services System, Nonesuch Acquisitions System, Purchase* (Ocelot), *Sydney*, and *Unicorn*. Additional notes on electronic ordering are also included.

Dewey, Patrick. *The Essential Guide to Bulletin Board Systems*. Meckler, 1987. Good news for anyone contemplating starting an electronic bulletin board service. Listed are dozens of software packages, with notes, extensive guidelines of things to avoid or remember, how to deal with hackers, and an extensive bibliography.

————. *The Essential Guide to the Library Apple: Volume 4, Software for Library Applications*. Meckler, 1987. Dozens of titles are outlined that can help libraries perform many of the projects listed.

————. *The Essential Guide to the Library IBM PC: Volume 4, Generic Software for Library Use*. Meckler, 1987. Approximately 100 software packages for general use are evaluated for their possible use in libraries.

————. *Microcomputers and the Reference Librarian*. Meckler, 1988. Provides hundreds of resources for answers to many reference questions about microcomputers, including software and hardware directories, games, bulletin boards, etc.

————. *101 Software Packages to Use in Your Library*. American Library Association, 1987. More than 100 software packages are reviewed and evaluated firsthand. Categories include cataloging and acquisitions packages, word processors, spreadsheets, database managers, circulation, interlibrary loan, bulletin board systems, and much more. Also includes listing of library microcomputer user groups.

————. *Public Access Microcomputers: A Handbook for Librarians*. 2d ed. G. K. Hall,

1990. Contains an overview of public access, with rules and guidelines as well as useful documents.

Goodman, Danny. *The Complete Hypercard Handbook.* Bantam, 1987. For anyone contemplating creating hypercard performances, this extensive handbook will prove essential, since it covers the commands in great detail, how to go about authoring a presentation, and much more.

Intner, Sheila and Hannigan, Jane Anne. *The Library Microcomputer Environment: Management Issues.* Oryx, 1988. Important areas of microcomputer management are explored by experts in the field. The topics include review sources for microcomputer materials, CD-ROM and satellite linkage, local area networking, organizing a collection of software, etc.

Melin, Nancy Jean. *The Essential Guide to the Library IBM PC: Volume 1, The Hardware Set-Up and Expansion.* Meckler, 1985. This first of a series of 15 volumes on the use of the IBM for library work helps the reader to make crucial decisions about hardware configurations, care and maintenance, and finding additional sources of information.

Milliot, Jim. *Micros at Work.* Knowledge Industry, 1985. Some 30 libraries are profiled regarding microcomputer use. The text does not deal with specific projects but discusses how micros have been integrated into the library setting.

Palmer, Roger C. *Online Reference and Information Retrieval.* 2d ed. Libraries Unlimited, 1987. In addition to a history of online services from the 1950s, many questions about such services are explored. A number of key areas in which decisions must be made or information gathered, along with resources for additional study, cover database producers, database indexing, authority and control, client interview, command language, search strategy, and trends and issues.

*The PC-SIG Library.* 4th ed. PC-SIG, 1987. Look for latest edition. PC-SIG is a national user group that offers high quality IBM public-domain and user-supported software at $4–6 per disk (user fees may be substantially more).

Polly, Jean Armour. *The Essential Guide to Apple Computers in Libraries: Volume 1, Public Technology: The Library Public Access Computer.* Polly discusses her highly successful public-access computer operation at the Liverpool (N.Y.) Public Library and how to solve many of the problems associated with walk-in use, circulation of software, etc. She also discusses the results of her survey of colleagues overseeing similar projects.

Valauskas, Edward J. *Macintoshed Libraries.* Apple Library Users Group, 1988. Contains several dozen excellent articles on the use of the Macintosh for library applications. Each article is written by a professional using a Mac in the library.

Walton, Robert. *Directory of Microcomputer Software for Libraries.* Oryx, 1986. While this volume does not contain any reviews, and the materials discussed are mostly those sent by the vendor, it is a valuable, comprehensive volume of basic information.

White, Howard S., ed. *Library Technology Reports.* American Library Association, Jan./Feb. 1986. This excellent volume assesses 16 major microcomputer circulation systems, listing prices, options, characteristics, and other valuable information.

# Serials

*Apple Library Users Group Newsletter,* 10380 Bandley Dr., Cupertino, CA 95014.

*Library Software Review,* Meckler Publishing Corporation, 11 Ferry Lane West, Westport, CT 06880.

*Computers in Libraries*, Meckler Publishing Corporation, 11 Ferry Lane West, Westport, CT 06880.

# Other Resources

Meckler Publishing Corporation has two excellent series of books: *The Essential Guide to the Library IBM PC* (15 volumes) and *The Essential Guide to Apple Computers in Libraries* (5 volumes).

# Index of Project Sites

Allegheny General Hospital 58
Apple Computer, Inc. 39, 87
Arlington Heights Memorial Library 18, 91

Beaver College, Atwood Library 11
Brighton High School 39
Brookens Library, Sangamon State University 105
Brunswick–Glynn County Regional Library 10

Chester County Library 92
College of Saint Scholastica Library 53
Colorado State University Libraries 55
Cullom–Davis Library, Bradley University 56

DALIS Automated Systems 112
Danville Area School District 34
Dublin Public Libraries 43
Duke University Law Library 16

East Carolina University, East Health Sciences Library 80
Educational Studies, University of Missouri–St. Louis 68
East Health Sciences Library, Carolina University 80
Elmhurst Public Library 51, 106
Evanston Public Library 40

Farrell Library, Kansas State University 64
Fenwick Library, George Mason University 47, 74

General Foods USA, Technical Information Center 30
Grace A. Dow Memorial Library 33
Graduate Library, University of Michigan 104
Grosse Pointe Public Library 122

Hagerty Library, Drexel University 109
Haydon Burns Library 110
Health Science Library, University of Tennessee 97
Health Sciences Library/SUNY at Buffalo 9
Hillsborough Community College 113

Indiana Youth Resources Information Network 126
Iowa State University, Music Listening Room 127

Johnson Elementary School Media Center 28

Kansas State Library 41
Kansas State University Libraries 35, 100
Kentucky Talking Book Library 61

Library, Department of Finance/Treasury Board of Canada 119
Lincoln High School 37
Liverpool Public Library 29,84
Lucy Hill Patterson Memorial Library 34
Lucy Scribner Library 82

Mankley Elementary School Library 26
Maywood Public Library 12, 23, 27, 38, 65, 67, 85, 89, 98, 107

147

Memorial Hall Library  86
Merriam Center Library  14, 16, 32, 42, 62,
    78, 79, 102
Methodist Hospitals of Memphis, Leslie M.
    Stratton Nursing Library  114
MMI Preparatory School  115
Music Library, University of Colorado  124

Nepean Public Library, Canada  101
North–Pulaski Branch Library/Chicago
    Public Library  21,90
Northwestern Regional Library  117

Ohio State University Health Sciences
    Library  77
Oregon Health Sciences University Librar-
    ies  62

Parlin–Ingersoll Public Library  88
Pennsylvania State Library  72
Pennsylvania State University  123
Phoenix Public Library  49

Richter Library, University of Miami  46

Sage Learning Center Library, Bronx Com-
    munity College  69
Salt Lake County Library System  96

San Jose Public Library  73
Seminole Community College Library  26
Shelby State Community College  53
State University of New York at Buffalo  8
Stockton–San Joaquin County Public
    Library  17
Suburban Library System  23
Sulzer Regional Library  13, 43
Surrattsville High School  108

Texas State Law Library  24
Texas Tech University Library  124
Torrance Public Library  92

University of California–Irvine, Biomedi-
    cal Library  22
University of California–Santa Cruz  63
University of Florida Libraries  121
University of Miami Library  47
University of Missouri  71
University of Wisconsin  104
Upland Public Library  94

Whitmore, Salt Lake County Library Sys-
    tem  96
Winston–Dillard Public School District
    #116  75
Wisconsin Interlibrary Services  56

# Index of Applications and Software

ACCESS PENNSYLVANIA CD-ROM database 72
Acquisitions 9
*Advanced Netware* 60
Apple Library Users Group 3
*AppleTerm* 123
*AppleWorks* 10, 18, 28, 33, 34, 53, 65, 75, 101, 116, 123
*AppleWriter* 10
*Art Roundup* 40

*BEX* 49
*BiblioFile Catalog Production System* 113
Bibliographies 12–15
*Bibliography Writer* 12, 117
Budget 11, 16–19
Bulletin Boards (Electronic) 20–25, 56

*CalendarMaker* 40
*Cards* 127
Career Guidance 106
Catalog Cards 67–76
CD-ROM 67, 72, 108
Circulation of Hardware 86
Circulation of Software 29, 35, 87, 89, 91
*Circulation Plus* 28, 116
Circulation System 26, 28, 30, 34, 60
*Click Art Publications* 37
*Clipper* 112, 126
Collection Analysis 63
Community Resource Directory 43
*COMPULOG* 70
*COMPULOG MEDIA* 70
CompuVend 109

*Data Factory* 98
*Datalog: Acquisitions* 59
*Datalog: Catalog* 59
*Datalog: Serials* 59
*DB Master* 10
*dBase II* 9, 13, 16, 43, 59
*dBase III* 11, 41, 47, 56, 73, 112
*dBase III+* 9, 11, 33, 69, 80, 97, 100, 117, 126
*dBase IV* 10
Desk Schedules 40
Desktop Publishing 37
Dialog Interface 78
*DoubleDOS* 57
*DUTalk* 109

*Edibase* 119
*Enable* 63

*FileMaker Plus* 26
*FileTalk* 49
*Finder* 51
*Fleet Street Editor Desktop Publisher* 44
Fliers 37
*Framework II* 62
*FYI-MCD* 25

*GBBS-Pro* 24
*GOVDOC* 47
Government Documents 46–48

Handicapped Accessibility 49
*HyperCard* 39

Indexing
 Keyword  47
 Pamphlet File  53
 Sheet Music  124
*inLARGE*  49
Interlibrary Loan  55
Inventory  60, 117

*Kermit*  42
Knowledge of Retrieval System  108
*KWICIE*  47

*Librarian's Helper*  67
Library Tour  39
Literacy  110
Local Area Networks (LAN)  58
Local History  51, 65
*Lotus 1-2-3*  40, 82

MacDraw  40
*MacPaint*  37, 50
*MacTerminal*  42, 109, 123
*MacWrite*  37, 42, 49, 104
Magazine Index  96
Management  62–66
MARC  71
Media Catalog  68, 74, 75
*MicroInterpreter I and II*  49
*MicroPhone 1.1*  79
*Microsoft File 1.05*  14, 63, 103
*Microsoft Word 3.01*  14, 40, 42
Modem  4

*Netware*  58
Newsletters  39, 42, 63
*Newsroom*  116
*Nutshell Database*  44

*Ocelot Library System*  113
OCLC  79, 100
Online Catalog  67–73
Overdues  26

*PageMaker*  40
Pamphlet Database  53
Pamphlet File  53
Patron Count Analysis  82
*People's Message System*  21
Periodicals  101, 102
*Personal Librarian* (formerly *SIRE*)  74

*PFS* series  34, 69
Posters  38
*Print Shop*  38
*Profile*  125
*Prokey*  40
Public Access  84–93
Public Domain Circulation  89, 91

*Quick Card*  116
*Quick File*  10
*Quickindex*  31
*Quicksilver*  112

*READS*  60
*RBBS*  57
*RBBS-PC CPC12.1A*  23
*RBBS-PC CPC16.1A*  23
*Red Ryder*  123
Résumé Preparation  104
Retrospective Conversion  44

Salary Increases  62
*ScreenTalk*  49
*ScreenTalk Pro*  49
*Search Helper*  96
Search Management  77
Security  5
Serials  100
*Sideways*  40
*Smart Database*  68
Space Planning  63
Stack Management  64
Staff Training  121
Star  45
Statistics  80
Subscriber Files  62
Summer Reading Clubs  94
*SuperCalc2*  17
*SuperCalc3*  64
*Sydney Micro Library System*  114
*System of Interactive Guidance and Testing*  106

Table of Contents  97
Templates  41

User Groups  3, 119, 122

*Vacalist*  51
Videotape List  27, 33

*VisiCalc*  18, 62
*VolksWriter 3*  73

Wall Charts  98
*WordPerfect*  49, 65

*WordStar 1512*  44
*WordTalk*  49, 54
Workshops  90

Patrick Dewey is director of the Maywood (Illinois) Public Library and also teaches an introductory course in microcomputer applications at Rosary College's Graduate Library School. He is the author of *101 Software Packages to Use in Your Library* (ALA, 1987).